T0213518

SpringerBriefs in Computer Science

More information about this series at http://www.springer.com/series/10028

Telmo Adão · Luís Magalhães
Emanuel Peres

Ontology-based Procedural Modelling of Traversable Buildings Composed by Arbitrary Shapes

 Springer

Telmo Adão
Department of Engineering
University of Trás-os-Montes e Alto Douro
 (UTAD)
Vila Real
Portugal

Emanuel Peres
Department of Engineering
INESC TEC (formerly INESC Porto) and
 University of Trás-os-Montes e Alto
 Douro (UTAD)
Vila Real
Portugal

Luís Magalhães
Department of Information Systems
ALGORITMI Center, University of Minho
 (UM)
Guimarães
Portugal

ISSN 2191-5768   ISSN 2191-5776   (electronic)
SpringerBriefs in Computer Science
ISBN 978-3-319-42371-5   ISBN 978-3-319-42372-2   (eBook)
DOI 10.1007/978-3-319-42372-2

Library of Congress Control Number: 2016947770

Printed on acid-free paper

This Springer imprint is published by Springer Nature
The registered company is Springer International Publishing AG
The registered company address is: Gewerbestrasse 11, 6330 Cham, Switzerland

Contents

Chapter 1
Introduction

Abstract Most of the existing procedural modelling solutions still lacks from support to the generation of virtual buildings with both exteriors and interiors composed by arbitrary shapes. To address this issue, a new procedural modelling methodology is presented in this book, one that produces virtual models of buildings, including exteriors outlined by arbitrary shapes and interiors formed by convex polygons. Regarding this specific chapter, some relevant subjects that define the boundaries of this book are introduced along with the motivation and goals that lie at the basis of the new methodology. Afterwards, a list of main contributions and assumptions are presented, shortly before book organization section.

3D virtual models of buildings are commonly used in areas such as architecture and video games to preview a house project and to populate a virtual scenario, respectively. Traditionally, the production of these models requires highly skilled manpower and a considerable amount of time. To address this issue, many researchers have developed semi-automatic techniques to produce virtual models expeditiously. These procedural techniques provide different ways of generating buildings, including interiors and outer facades, to serve several purposes (e.g., content generation for video games or archaeological reconstruction). However, the existing techniques focusing on building interiors usually only support the generation of floor plans constrained by regular shapes or contour polygons obtained from rectangles sets. At the same time, the possibility of modelling interior rooms through the specification of its constraint walls remains poorly explored. Moreover, most of the existing procedural generation solutions are guided by complex grammars concerned with geometrical aspects or semantic structures that fit specific project requirements, apparently disregarding the established standards for virtual urban environments, specifically, CityGML.

To overcome the noted issues, a novel procedural modelling methodology is presented in this book, one that produces virtual models of buildings, including exteriors outlined by arbitrary shapes and interiors formed by convex polygons. Methodology's regulation is provided by a building ontology—a CityGML-based knowledge structure [1, 2], planned to be extensible to specific architecture styles— through several guiding data structures such as structured XML and ontology-based

© The Author(s) 2016

T. Adão et al., *Ontology-based Procedural Modelling of Traversable*
Buildings Composed by Arbitrary Shapes, SpringerBriefs in Computer Science,
DOI 10.1007/978-3-319-42372-2_1

grammar. Regarding the supporting process, a treemap approach is used to subdivide the building layout into floor plan areas. Several improvements were progressively made to the treemap in order to enable the subdivision of different constraint polygon types which range from rectangles to arbitrary shapes. Moreover, in the most advanced methodology stage, a method concerning inner room walls adaptation is addressed. Next, a set of operations is performed, from the marking transitions step to the extrusion process that provides the 3D aspect. In addition, an experimental stochastic approach is shown to automate the production of random buildings using this procedural modelling methodology.

Nearby the end of the book, a set of tests to evaluate the capabilities of the referred methodology in producing buildings characterized by arbitrary shapes and distinct architectonic requirements will be presented. Furthermore, the results of the performance tests will be shown.

Regarding this specific chapter, a few subjects will be introduced, concretely the production of contents for virtual environments, procedural modelling and also ontologies. Those subjects constitute the boundaries of this book which has its motivation and goals presented shortly afterwards along with some assumptions. This chapter ends with the main contributions and orientations regarding document organization.

1.1 Content Production for Virtual Environments

Content production for virtual environments is an important subject as it is directly related with parameters such as production cost and development time, which have a significant impact in how well a business or research performs. The conventional production of these models—specifically, using manual modelling—requires highly skilled manpower and a considerable amount of time to achieve the desired virtual contents, in a process composed by many stages that are typically repeated over time.

As technology continues to evolve at a faster rate—more processing power, faster and larger memory, increased disk space at better r/w rates and more powerful graphic boards—new paradigms are emerging to provide more efficient and cost-effective solutions for business that depend on virtual contents. Among them is procedural modelling which can be seen as an assortment of techniques that aim to automatize the production of virtual models through the assimilation of patterns and algorithmic approaches that assume the role of content production engines. From the perspective of some business and research areas (e.g. architecture, archaeology, videogames producers), the overwhelming use of resources can now be drastically reduced, leading to the increase of competitiveness. Moreover, man-skilled labour can now be concentrated in the validation and improvement of the automatically produced models by adding or altering particularities and details that might make them closer to the expected results, considering the requirements of a given modelling task in a certain context.

The application fields are numerous. Videogames industry is perhaps one of the most obvious cases, due to the use of complex road networks and rich urban environments, pretty noticeable in games, such as Grand Theft Auto (GTA)[1] or Need For Speed (NFS).[2] Actually, NFS was a case study for Watson et al. [3] who had underlined the applicability and importance of procedural modelling in the production of certain game contents, such as buildings and road networks, due to its cost-effective and dynamic nature. Moreover, they suggest that designers who demand for automatic ways of generating game contents to avoid tedious and repetitive hand-made tasks, can be supported by procedural modelling tools to generate the first set of urban objects, that afterwards can be customized to make them look like what they have projected.

The same modelling style can be used in the archaeological research area, even in damaged structures—as it is pointed out by Müller et al. [4], Rodrigues et al. [5] or Dylla et al. [6]—to aid, for example, in the proposal of hypothesis that can be valuable for the formulation of theories among that scientific community.

Another application field is 3D cinema. Enterprises like Pixar[3] or Dreamworks Animation[4] are specialized in producing 3D movies that include human and animal characters, cities, villages and forests. Some of their productions already take advantage from procedural modelling techniques. For example, in the Monters Inc. (Pixar) movie, the hair of Sulley character is procedurally animated [7]. Another example is the fracturing and debris procedural technique that was developed for Kung-Fu Panda (Dreamworks) in order to be applied in several scenes involving massive destruction of structures [8].

These were just a few examples intending to show procedural modelling versatility. However, others will be provided in the next chapters, to demonstrate the wide range of applicability of this modelling style in the generation of structures—specifically, buildings—expeditiously and demanding low user interaction.

1.2 Main Concepts

The concepts inherent to the areas addressed in this book will be presented, namely, ontologies and procedural modelling. Building Information Modelling (BIM) disambiguation closes the section.

---

[1]Grand Theft Auto, also known as GTA, is a well-known role playing game series, developed by Rockstar. For more information, check the link: http://www.rockstargames.com/grandtheftauto/.

[2]Need For Speed or NFS, is a racing game series developed by Electronic Arts. For more information, check the link: http://www.needforspeed.com/.

[3]Pixar is a digital animation enterprise that belongs to the Walt Disney Company. For more information, check the link: http://www.pixar.com/.

[4]Dreamworks Animation is a north-american studio specialized in animation movies. For more information, check the link: http://www.dreamworksanimation.com/.

1.2.1   Production of Buildings Using Procedural Modelling

The production of buildings and urban environments are major concerns for the procedural modelling area. Many works [6, 9–11] present different approaches for the procedural generation of extensive urban environments, considering the exterior facades. These solutions have demonstrated to be a reliable alternative to manual approaches, since they are also capable of producing representations endowed with high levels of detail and visual accuracy. Regarding time consumption, the procedural solutions are incomparably faster. The same conclusions are valid for the generation of buildings considering their interiors [5, 12–14] which proposes the fully production of such structures including exterior facades, inner rooms and also the transitions that ensure transitivity among them.

1.2.2   Regulation Through Ontologies

Ontologies are knowledge structures capable of describing a system, namely the relations between its parts. They have been successfully applied in different solutions that require the use of virtual models/environments [15–17] to achieve a wide variety of purposes that range from the planning of neurosurgery operation to the cataloguing of museum artefacts. A few procedural modelling solutions also used them to guide the process of generating virtual models [13, 18, 19]. The results are interesting. However, most of these procedural modelling solutions seem confined to the context for which they were developed, disregarding standards oriented for virtual environments.

1.2.3   Ontology-Based Procedural Modelling Versus Building Information Modelling

This subsection intends to clarify the main differences between ontology-based procedural modelling approach and Building Information Modelling (BIM) which, due to the common use of semantics and similar goals, are liable to cause confusion.

BIM supports the development and use of a computer-generated model to simulate the different stages of a facility such as planning design and construction. Its preciseness, flexibility and huge range of possibilities make it suitable for construction professionals [20]. It is a complex standard that mixes semantic and geometry and contains a complete set of information—including, for example, the air conditioning system, the building structure or even the materials of its walls—and which requires expertise and labour when dealing with it, in order to meet client requirements and also legal and physical rules.

On the other hand, ontology-based procedural modelling is concerned with the rapidly and faithful visualization of virtual structures, disregarding imperceptible details—such as the skeleton structure of a building—which can be harmful to the fluidity that is required, for example, in a video-game. During the exploration of a virtual scenario, these details are usually not needed for observation. Thereby, the performance issues are avoided at two levels: in the structures generation for further visualization; and in the virtual environment navigation itself that is only provided with required contents for visualization, possibly using a level-of-detail (LOD) loading strategy for computational resources management purposes.

Regarding the requirements of this procedural modelling solution, a CityGML-based ontology was adopted and consists in a semantic structure simpler than BIM semantics, as it will be detailed in later sections. This option does not reject the possibility of having the resulting models integrated in BIM-based projects, since one of the CityGML [1, 2] concerns is to improve the interoperability between the referred construction standard and urban virtual environments [21].

1.3   Motivation and Goals

Real-world buildings are made up of very diverse geometries. Probably, the most commonly found sustaining floor plans are based on rectangular shapes. However, many contemporaneous and historical buildings have layouts composed by wider sets of geometries, like the ones depicted in Fig. 1.1.

Currently, procedural modelling methodologies to specifically deal with traversable buildings composed by non-square-based polygons—such as the ones presented in Fig. 1.1—including interiors (i.e. delimiting room walls) and exteriors (i.e. constraint building limits) are scarce. Moreover, notwithstanding the available and complete procedural modelling methodologies, some issues were identified:

- currently, the generation of virtual buildings with interior divisions composed by a customized number of constraint walls is poorly explored;
- most of the approaches generating virtual buildings only operate with constraint polygons based on rectangles;
- the absence of a semantic organization into a comprehensive and extensive ontology (or similar) based on standards—which is noticed in most of the procedural modelling solutions—might difficult the derivation of new architectonic styles and the exchange of information among heterogeneous systems regarding virtual environments, in general.

Thus, considering the aforementioned issues, the main goal of this book is to present a methodology capable of producing traversable buildings internally and externally described by more shapes than the rectangular-based ones. Moreover, in order to guide the referred methodology through the modelling of multiple structures belonging to different architectonic styles (e.g. ancient roman style, neoclassic, post-modern), a flexible and extensible ontology is also presented. It relies in CityGML [1, 2] which is an extensive and mature standard for virtual urban environments that

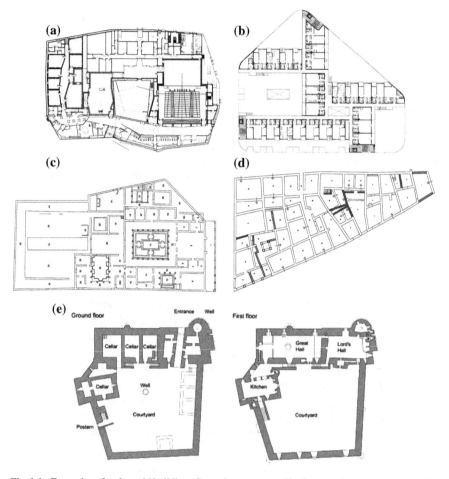

Fig. 1.1 Examples of real-world buildings floor plans composed by inner and outer non-rectangular shapes: **a** Paloma music complex, Nantes, France [22]; **b** SZA residential and business center, Zagreb, Croatia [23]; **c** House of Cantaber and **d** Insula of the Phallus vase ruins, Coimbra, Portugal [24]; **e** Doune Castle, Doune Village, Scotland [25] (adapted from [26])

documents a set of data models, including the generic composition and organization of the building entity. Summing up, the specific goals of this book are the following:

- Identify the limitations that currently affect the procedural modelling research area;
- Present a novel methodology, capable of overcoming the identified issues;
- Demonstrate the software prototype that was implemented to evaluate both effectiveness and performance of the referred methodology;
- Provide a succinct discussion about the obtained results and compare them with other relevant works.

1.4 Main Contributions

This book intends to address the aforementioned issues regarding the procedural modelling area, by providing the following contributions:

- Presentation of a new procedural modelling methodology capable of producing traversable buildings constrained by arbitrary convex shapes, based on a pure treemap approach;
- Establishment of a process to change the format of the interior rooms, through wall number modification;
- Adaptation of a "fake-concave" technique to support non-convex buildings layouts;
- Definition of an extensible building ontology to guide the methodology process and support the generation of other architectural style buildings (e.g. roman houses);
- Presentation of a few ontology-based structures—eXtensible Markup Language (XML) and ontological grammar—to provide the procedural modelling methodology with production rules;
- Outlining of computer-managed processes for the stochastic generation of buildings;
- Demonstration of results produced in a toolkit that implements the above-mentioned procedural modelling methodology and computer-managed processes for automating building production.

1.5 Assumptions

This section will present a set of topics that the reader must take into consideration, when consulting this book. They will help to clarify which aspects are addressed and which are not:

- The procedural modelling methodology presented in this book will only focus on the generation of buildings with one floor, despite the support of the ontology to achieve more than that;
- The methodology aims the generation of individual buildings that can possibly be integrated in more extensive urban environments;
- The methodology intends to be an alternative for the existing ones and aims to produce a wider range of structures described by an extensive range of geometries, rather than to be concerned with faithful architectonic representations;
- Most of the generated models follow a deterministic approach. However, a stochastic alternative for the fully automated productions of buildings is glimpsed, constituting a preliminary approach devoid of real architectonic regulation;
- Slanted walls will not be addressed;
- When discussing the methodology, the term "room" is sometimes applied as having the same meaning as "division", which is formally characterized in the ontology addressed on Chap. 3;

- All of the implementation versions regarding the modelling methodology were made under Microsoft's .NET framework,[5] using C# programming language[6] and also the XNA framework[7];
- This book focus the procedural modelling of buildings, not the rendering aspects. To visualize the created models, a XNA-based previewer was developed and a Blender software[8] was used.

1.6 Book Organization

Besides the introduction, this book is constituted by seven other chapters.

Chapter 2 addresses ontologies and its effective applications on several fields requiring virtual models and environments. Also, an extensive revision targeting the state-of-the-art on procedural modelling is presented and its main contents include urban environments, traversable buildings and ontological approaches.

The third chapter (Chap. 3) presents an overview of the procedural modelling methodology for generating building's outlined and internally composed by arbitrary shapes.

Chapters 4–6 will expose in detail each development and implementation stage of the methodology. Chapter 4 addresses a first approach, which joins ontology and treemaps to achieve the creation of roman houses—uniquely composed by square shapes. Some improvements will be presented in Chap. 5 which focus the generation of traversable buildings constrained by convex shapes. The final version of the procedural modelling methodology that aims the semi- or automatic generation of buildings constrained by non-convex shapes and composed by interior rooms with a variable wall number will be addressed in the sixth chapter (Chap. 6) which ends with the presentation of a toolkit implementing that methodology.

The methodology evaluation is addressed in the seventh chapter (Chap. 7), using the aforementioned toolkit. Several tests will be presented regarding the generation of structures and computational performance.

The final chapter—Chap. 8—ends this document by exposing the conclusions, a brief discussion and some final remarks.

---

[5]Microsoft .NET framework refers to a collection of programming libraries that enables the use of .NET platform functionalities (link: http://www.microsoft.com/net).

[6]C# is a powerful and flexible object-oriented programming language developed by Microsoft. More informations are available at the link: https://msdn.microsoft.com/en-us/library/kx37x362.aspx.

[7]Microsoft XNA (not acronymed) framework is a software development kit for game production dedicated to Microsoft compatible devices (PC, Xbox). For more information, consult the following link: http://msdn.microsoft.com/xna.

[8]Blender is a free and professional computer-aided design (CAD) software developed, maintained and distributed by Blender Foundation. It is used for 3D modelling, UV wrapping, texturing, raster graphics editing and others (link: http://www.blender.org).

References

1. Gröger, G., Kolbe, T.H., Czerwinski, A., Nagel, C.: OGC City Geography Markup Language (CityGML) Encoding Standard. Technical report, Open Geospatial Consortium (2008)
2. Gröger, G., Kolbe, T.H., Nagel, C., Häfele, K.-H.: OGC City Geography Markup Language (CityGML) Encoding Standard. Technical report, Open Geospatial Consortium (2012)
3. Watson, B., Muller, P., Wonka, P., Sexton, C., Veryovka, O., Fuller, A.: Procedural urban modeling in practice. IEEE Comput. Graph. Appl. **28**(3), 18–26 (2008). ISSN 0272-1716. doi:10.1109/MCG.2008.58
4. Müller, P., Vereenooghe, T., Wonka, P., Paap, I., Van Gool, L.: Procedural 3d reconstruction of puuc buildings in xkipché. In: Eurographics Symposium on Virtual Reality, Archaeology and Cultural Heritage (VAST), pp. 139–146. EG (2006)
5. Rodrigues, N., Dionísio, M., Gonçalves, A., Magalhães, L.M.G., Moura, J.P.: Rule-based generation of houses. Comput. Graph. Geom. **10**(2), 49–65 (2008). http://cgg-journal.com /2008-2/05/index.html
6. Dylla, K., Muller, P., Ulmer, A., Haegler, S., Fischer, B.: Rome reborn 2.0: a case study of virtual city reconstruction using procedural modeling techniques. In: Proceedings of Computer Applications and Quantitative Methods in Archaeology (2009)
7. Cohen, K., Monsters, Inc.: The secret behind why pixar is so good. Animation World Mag. (6), 6–12 (2001)
8. Lee, L., Pavlov, N., DreamWorks Animation: Procedural fracturing and debris generation for kung-fu panda. In: ACM SIGGRAPH 2008 Talks, pp. 59. ACM (2008)
9. Parish, Y.I.H., Müller, P.: Procedural modeling of cities. In: Proceedings of the 28th Annual Conference on Computer Graphics and Interactive Techniques, SIGGRAPH '01, pp. 301–308, New York, NY, USA, 2001. ACM (2001). ISBN 1-58113-374-X. doi:10.1145/383259.383292
10. Müller, P., Wonka, P., Haegler, S., Ulmer, A., Van Gool, L.: Procedural modeling of buildings. ACM Trans. Graph. **25**(3), 614–623 (2006). ISSN 0730-0301. doi:10.1145/1141911.1141931
11. Silva, P.B., Coelho, A.: Procedural modeling for realistic virtual worlds development. J. Virtual Worlds Res. **4**(1) (2011). doi:10.4101/jvwr.v4i1.2109. https://journals.tdl.org/jvwr/index.php/ jvwr/article/view/2109/5541
12. Marson, F., Musse, S.R.: Automatic real-time generation of floor plans based on squarified treemaps algorithm. Int. J. Comput. Games Technol. **2010**, 7:1–7:10 (2010). ISSN 1687-7047. doi:10.1155/2010/624817
13. Tutenel, T., Smelik, R.M., Lopes, R., de Kraker, K.J., Bidarra, R.: Generating consistent buildings: a semantic approach for integrating procedural techniques. IEEE Trans. Comput. Intell. AI Games **3**(3), 274–288 (2011). ISSN 1943-068X. doi:10.1109/TCIAIG.2011.2162842
14. Merrell, P., Schkufza, E., Koltun, V.: Computer-generated residential building layouts. ACM Trans. Graph. **29**(6), 181:1–181:12 (2010). ISSN 0730-0301. doi:10.1145/1882261.1866203
15. Lee, J.Y., Seo, D.W., Rhee, G.: Visualization and interaction of pervasive services using context-aware augmented reality. Expert Syst. Appl. **35**(4), 1873–1882 (2008). ISSN 0957-4174. doi:10.1016/j.eswa.2007.08.092. http://www.sciencedirect.com/science/article/ pii/S0957417407003818
16. Attene, M., Robbiano, F., Spagnuolo, M., Falcidieno, B.: Characterization of 3d shape parts for semantic annotation. Comput.-Aided Des. **41**(10), 756–763 (2009)
17. Hunter, J., Gerber, A.: Harvesting community annotations on 3d models of museum artefacts to enhance knowledge, discovery and re-use. J. Cult. Herit. **11**(1), 81–90 (2010)
18. Liu, Y., Xu, C., Zhang, Q., Pan, Y.: The smart architect: scalable ontology-based modeling of ancient chinese architectures. IEEE Intell. Syst. **23**(1), 49–56 (2008). ISSN 1541-1672
19. Trescak, T., Esteva, M., Rodriguez, I.: A virtual world grammar for automatic generation of virtual worlds. Vis. Comput. **26**(6-8), 521–531 (2010). ISSN 0178-2789. doi:10.1007/s00371-010-0473-7
20. Azhar, S.: Building information modeling (BIM): trends, benefits, risks, and challenges for the AEC industry. Leadership Manag. Eng. **11**(3), 241–252 (2011)

21. Kolbe, T.H.: What is citygml? (2012). http://www.citygml.org/index.php?id=1533
22. TETRARC Architects: Paloma music complex in Nimes (2012). https://mir-s3-cdn-cf.
    behance.net/project_modules/disp/2f580c49280951.5608543b4bd2b.jpg. Accessed 2015
23. Studio za arhitekturu (SZA): SZA: residential and business center in zagreb (2010).
    http://www.designboom.com/cms/images/erica/----zagreb/zagreb13.gif. Accessed 2015
24. Correia, V.H.: A arquitectura doméstica de Conimbriga e as estruturas económicas e sociais
    da cidade romana, vol. 1. Coimbra, Instituto de Arqueologia, Anexos de Conimbriga 6, 2013.
    Representation of *Casa de Cantaber* (House of Cantaber, p. 99) and *Insula do Vaso Fálico*
    (Insula of the Phallus Vase, p. 134) floorplans, according to the author. Courtesy of Virgílio
    Hipólito Correia: director of the Museu Monográfico de Conimbriga (2013)
25. Jonathan Oldenbuck: Doune Castle (2008). https://en.wikipedia.org/wiki/Doune_Castle#/
    media/File:Doune_Castle_plan.png. Accessed 2015
26. Douglas Simpson, W.: Doune castle. In: Proceedings of the Society of Antiquaries of Scotland,
    vol. 72, pp. 73–83. Society of Antiquaries of Scotland (1938). http://archaeologydataservice.
    ac.uk/archives/view/psas/contents.cfm?vol=72

Chapter 2
Ontologies and Procedural Modelling

Abstract This chapter consists of a literature review regarding the use of ontologies on virtual environments and the procedural modelling solutions that have been proposed with focus in two approaches: (1) the production of virtual hollow buildings, uniquely composed by outer facades; and (2) the production of virtual traversable buildings, with interior divisions included. The integration of ontologies and semantics in procedural modelling is also addressed in each one of the referred approaches.

2.1 Ontologies on Virtual Environments

Over the years, several authors [12–14] have defined and characterized "ontology" while others [15–17] were concerned with its applications in fields such as information systems and engineering. All of them inspired Guarino [18] and Chandrasekaran et al. [19] in the formulation of their own concepts about these knowledge organization structures.

According to Guarino [18], an ontology aims to describe a certain entity using a particular system of categories. In some areas like engineering—such as Artificial Intelligence—an ontology is established through a set of concepts and respective meanings (i.e. vocabulary) with a relation structure that intends to characterize a certain reality. The author also refers the increasing importance of ontologies for computer science, focusing in the information systems area, in which ontologies can play an important role due to their straight relation with components such as databases and program objects and application programs.

Chandrasekaran et al. [19], shares a similar vision. The author states that this kind of structures intends to represent a set of facts related with a particular domain through the organization of the integrating knowledge concepts. This organization arises from the analysis over the domain fields, in which the following authors' assumption should be considered:

> Weak analyses lead to incoherent knowledge bases.
> —Chandrasekaran et al. [19]

© The Author(s) 2016   11
T. Adão et al., *Ontology-based Procedural Modelling of Traversable
Buildings Composed by Arbitrary Shapes*, SpringerBriefs in Computer Science,
DOI 10.1007/978-3-319-42372-2_2

One of the most interesting features of ontologies is the possibility of sharing knowledge. This promotes a re-usability and standardization. For example, a building can share characteristics common in several architectonic styles. Despite their appearance on the different styles, a window, a door and a wall are transversal elements to the majority of the existing architectonic styles. The representation of particular cases (e.g. Manueline window, mesquite entrance, skylight) are extensions of the generic ones.

> Shared ontologies let us build specific knowledge bases
> that describe specific situations.
> —Chandrasekaran et al. [19]

Besides re-usability, ontologies are considered, by Chandrasekaran et al. [19], abstract structures. The combination of these two features are completely compatible with the design of data models and object oriented programming classes (towards the considerations made by Guarino [18]). Thus, the ontological analysis of a certain domain field can be suitable for integration in areas such as computer science and software engineering, for both project stages: requirement analysis and algorithmic development.

Considering the notions left by Guarino [18] and Chandrasekaran et al. [19] at an abstract level, one can infer that the use of ontologies can be extended to other areas—besides information systems or software engineering—namely the ones involving virtual representations, as some authors have already shown (e.g. [20–22]). The following subsections will expose some of the works that successfully applied ontologies to regulate virtual representations in different scenarios and contexts. CityGML standard will also be discussed, due to its relevance in the context of virtual environments representation.

2.1.1 Virtual Representations Based on Ontologies

The integration of ontologies in some of the works developed around virtual representations will be presented in this subsection. Although the concept of ontology has been explored for a while, this way of structuring knowledge is still largely used by several authors today.

Pittarello and De Faveri [23] were concerned with the lack of semantic description across the considerable amount of virtual environments available on the Internet, which prevented a proper interaction with them. To get around this issue by enhancing the models with semantics, the authors proposed a solution capable of relating geometric primitives—X3D and VRML—with semantic class objects through the so called *MetadataSet* nodes. An independent scene ontology was also incorporated to establish a set of relations used for the description of a certain domain (for example, a wall can be contained inside the room).

One year later, an approach involving surgical models for computer-assisted neurosurgery was proposed by Jannin and Morandi [20]. The aim of this work is to provide a visual framework for planning surgeries, improving human–computer interfaces—specifically, for the computer-assisted surgery systems—thus formalizing the surgical knowledge and practice. The presented framework relies in a surgical ontology which establishes the concepts and relationships belonging to the surgical work domain—extensible to other areas of medicine—and a supporting software that describes the surgical procedures.

For setting up urban environments, a work that employs ontologies was proposed by García-Rojas et al. [24]. Their parametric system allows common users—nonexperts in the virtual reality field—to prepare 3D scenes through an on-demand configuration. To achieve this, a visual programming paradigm, supported by a proper ontology, allows the organization of a 3D scene components.

A pervasive system, proposed by Lee et al. [25], combines ontology-based context-awareness with adaptable augmented reality. In short, the framework considers several aspects such as user preferences, device profiles and security to augment personalized virtual models, which must in accordance with a given acquired context. Context-awareness is provided by three ontologies. The first ontology holds the general concepts related with the pervasive environment. A second ontology organizes knowledge about users' device profile (related with the mobile device capabilities) and preferences (a set of user options). At last, a social ontology maps users activities related with information shared in the web, for further re-utilization. The authors exposed three system applications as examples: ubiquitous home visualization and simulation, ubiquitous car services and ubiquitous engineering collaboration.

The strength of ontologies was once again highlighted by ShapeAnnotator: a system developed by Attene et al. [21] that allows the classification of 3D virtual model meshes in a certain knowledge domain. The system provides a set of tools for model segmentation that can be manipulated by a user in order to easy and properly link the model parts to the domain knowledge, formalized by an ontology. The usefulness of ShapeAnnotator framework was discussed in two scenarios. The first one explains the potentialities of the tool in supporting the creation of human models (avatars) for Multi-massive online role playing games (MMORPGs) and virtual worlds, such as Second Life. The second scenario focuses the collaborative e-manufacturing of 3D products taking advantage from the abstractness and re-usability provided by the ontology.

In the museums context, another system assisted by ontologies that aims the collaborative annotations of 3D museum artifacts through web-based services, was proposed [26]. This system—entitled Harvesting and Aggregating Networked Annotations (HarvANA)—promotes the participation of communities in the cultural enrichment and improves museum objects indexation. One of the most relevant features of this system is the flexible ontology-based categorization—called of folksonomy—which optimizes tagging proceedings among the communities.

In the context of urban planning and management, Martins [27] proposed an urban ontology to overcome the issue of data heterogeneity among municipalities that use different geographic information data sources. The main idea is to establish a common data model and provide an unified platform for data sharing between municipal technicians. Thereby, the author supported a significant part of his work in the CityGML standard—addressed in the next subsection—to develop a set of data models, which intend to reflect the different urban elements. For example, the proposed building model establishes a structure which includes a building, building parts, rooms, openings such as doors and windows and several boundary surfaces like walls, grounds, ceilings and furniture.

A couple of years later, Colledani et al. [28] proposed the integration of several heterogeneous software tools for manufacturing activity design over the same platform, using ontologies for uniformization purposes. This is implemented through the so-called Virtual Factory Framework, which is composed by several components: data and knowledge, Semantic Virtual Factory Data Model (VFDM), Semantic Virtual Factory Manager (VFM), decoupled virtual factory modules and the real factory interface. In this case, the VFDM is the abstraction layer holding the ontology that can extend products and define manufacturing processes. The rest of the components complete the system by ensuring the connection of the framework to the external applications, through special framework connectors designed for integration.

Recently, Flotynski [29] developed the Semantic Modelling of Interactive 3D Content (SEMIC), which employs a method for the modelling of knowledge, rather than the modelling of virtual content itself. SEMIC employs a method that consists in the mapping of 3D content into semantic classes, which are related with each other, in order to establish object relations for a given domain. The creation of 3D content consists in a set of well-defined steps that includes the design of the concrete semantic representation containing properties related with the 3D content, the mapping of specific domain concepts and the design of a conceptual semantic representation of 3D content, for arbitrary 3D creation purposes. These steps, as the author refers, require the intervention of different skilled professionals such as content developers, domain experts and content consumers. This aspect might suggest that this system is somewhat complex regarding 3D virtual models creation process.

Another recent approach addressing simulations in virtual environments was proposed by Béhé et al. [22]. The authors presented a framework for interactive multiagent-based simulations in virtual environments, adapting ontologies as a core notion to ease the simulation design and re-usability. Thereby, simulations are configurable through semantic modelling. This is used to describe the different aspects of the simulation, namely agent behaviours, surrounding environments with physical objects, scheduling for operation progress and the results of agent actions and interactions.

The differences between Geographical Information Systems (GIS) and BIM were addressed by Mignard and Nicolle [30], who developed a system called SIGA3D. This system takes advantage of ontologies, to provide interoperability between construction and urban management. So, information about buildings and geographic data can be managed together, in the same structure. The system also promotes collaboration between facility managers, aiming the enrichment of knowledge models since the designing stage to buildings' recycling.

The last work reviewed in this subsection is Virtual Collaboration Arena (VirCA): a collaborative virtual/augmented reality framework that enables testing and training events in the context of manufacturing systems, through several practical scenarios [31]. Such scenarios are mounted through web-based applications and interfaces that provide mechanisms for using and extending virtual reality content. Interaction with the referred scenarios is provided by cyber devices, also known as CDs, that enable the manipulation of their objects. The ontology concept acts here: a semantic manager layer ensures the bidirectional communication between CDs and virtual scenes, factoring on the available capabilities and requests—in terms of allowed actions/functionalities—supplied by the scenes' ontologies.

Summing up, one might conclude that ontologies have made a significant contribution to the success of several works, some of them referred in this subsection. This way of organizing knowledge to regulate processes has revealed robustness and flexibility in several works that require data representation through virtual models in a wide variety of contexts such as simulation, industrial manufacturing, collaboration, urban planning and others. However, in the specific context of 3D urban modelling, there is a well-defined urban knowledge structuring standard named CityGML. The next subsection will address some of the most relevant features of this standard.

2.1.2   CityGML: A 3D Urban Environment Standard

CityGML is, perhaps, the most important effort for the standardization of 3D urban representations [32, 33]. These guidelines, proposed by the Open Geospatial Consortium (OCG), intend to provide a widespread XML-based format for the geometric and semantic representations of city components. The standard covers the building entity including its inner and outer components. Kolbe [34] explains the CityGML support to this crucial city element, by presenting also an abstract class named of _AbstractBuilding. This is the mother class that derives to *Building* and *Building-Part*. *Building* holds sets of *BuildingPart* which can be seen as groups of structures that take advantage of the recursive relation with the _AbstractBuilding in order to support a wider range of structural rearrangements. For example, a given building may hold a stack of floors and a castle might be constituted by a set of horizontal distinguishable parts such as towers, curtain walls or gatehouses. Buildings and building parts can be represented in terms of constraints by another important class which is the *BoundarySurface*. This one can derive to specific boundaries such as *WallSurface* or *RoofSurface*. Furthermore, this boundaries may hold a set of objects spawned from _Opening class, as for example, doors and windows. Finally, *Room* class is intended to support the inner compartments inside the building and building parts. The diagram that describes the building knowledge organization is depicted on Fig. 2.1.

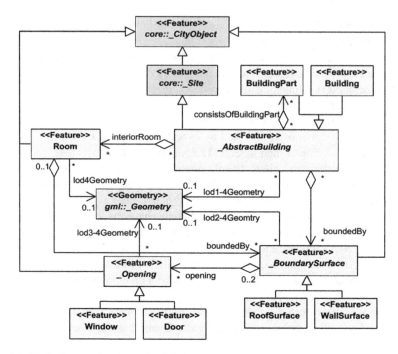

Fig. 2.1 UML diagram showing a simplified excerpt from the CityGML building model [34]

The specification of buildings is also extensively addressed by Industry Foundation Classes (IFC): a data model standard widely used by the construction industry for project purposes, in the context of BIM process [35]. However, the quantity of addressed civil construction and architectural domains [36] is excessive and technically complex to describe an urban environment oriented for areas such as videogames, 3D cinema or archaeology. The overload of dispensable information—not perceptible to the eye during representation—can even, in some cases, harm the objective of the virtual building representation, depending on usage context (unnecessary heavy and time consuming renderings, graphical lag, heavy processing, etc.). To conclude and considering such aspects, CityGML seems to be more suitable for designing general urban environments that target virtual content creation for areas as the ones that were aforementioned.

Besides the various applications of ontologies on virtual environments, some procedural modelling works also use them to regulate structures' generation (e.g.: [9, 11, 37–39]). The aforementioned works will be presented during the following pair of sections, which are reserved for an extensive analysis to procedural modelling, including the generation/reconstruction of virtual extensive urban environments and traversable buildings.

2.2 Procedural Modelling of Virtual Urban Environments

In this section, the production of virtual environments concerning the generation/reconstruction of exteriors will be presented. These environments are mainly composed by street networks and buildings, exclusively represented by outer facades.

2.2.1 L-Systems for Procedural Modelling

L-System was introduced by Lindenmayer [40] and adopted by Parish and Müller [1] to generate an extensive virtual environment considering its exterior layout. This technique uses an alphabet of symbols combined with a set of production rules. The process starts with an initial set of symbols that are iteratively replaced by other symbols until the final string is obtained. This final string is then used to generate shapes through a transformation mechanism. Parish and Müller [1] used this technique in two steps: one for generating a street network and other for producing buildings that can be described by several formats, provided by extrusion operations.

XL3D modelling system [41] also incorporates a geospatial L-System. Streets and blocks coordinates provided by a database populated with real data were used in combination with the L-System production rules, to generate the virtual downtown of Porto, Portugal.

2.2.2 Detailing Facades Through Split Grammars

Split grammar was introduced by Wonka et al. [2]. This technique relies on a grammar that operates in the context of a shape in order to produce 3D layouts. There are two types of rules in this grammar: splitting rules to replace geometries and conversion rules to produce transformations upon geometries. Shapes marked to be splitted or converted can be categorized in two classes: terminal and nonterminal. The process starts with an initial shape. A split grammar operates iteratively to force the shape to undergo several nonterminal states, until its final form. This process is considered finalized when all shapes in a pool reach their final state. Split grammar was applied to improve the details of building facades.

Later, Larive and Gaildrat [42], developed a wall grammar for buildings' generation, based on the split grammar of Wonka et al. [2]. This wall grammar integrates a technique to produce 3D buildings with exterior facades. The process encodes several elements—such as building footprint and height extracted from GIS, user specifications and high-level features for the building exterior appearance—into grammar rules that are applied to create a building with extruded walls representing outer facades. Differently from [2], this grammar operates on walls instead of shapes. Finally, a straight skeleton technique [43, 44] is used to generate the building's roofs.

2.2.3 Semi-automatic Digital Reconstruction of Old Buildings Considering GIS Data-Based Topology

A preserved area of Nicosia city was digitally reproduced through a partial automatic method which combines geographic data of building bases, building classification and style-concordant building components, such as doors and balconies [45]. Two distinct processes integrate the method. The former consists in photographing particular elements of the city to model realistic virtual building components. The later is a rule-based automatic process that starts by comparing the outline of each building—obtained from GIS data—with templates to determine building topology. Then, the ground edges are transformed into 3D walls. The previously modelled virtual building components are applied to each wall accordingly with the building topology classification and wall space available. Finally, using a straight skeleton computation approach [43, 46], the roof of each building is properly produced and applied.

2.2.4 Random Extrusion of Floors

Greuter et al. [47] proposed a system to generate pseudo-infinite cities. The generation of road networks is based on a regular grid, globally adjustable. The generation of buildings is achieved by combining geometric primitives—each set corresponds to a floor plan—that varies from floor to floor. The process starts with an elementary set of geometries, at the building top. Then, an extrusion forms a volume and primitives are added to a subsequent level. The process is repeated until reaching the building ground level.

2.2.5 Feature-Based Decomposition of Facades

Finkenzeller et al. [48] were capable of creating highly detailed realistic facades using floor plan modules (aggregations of 2D shapes at the ground level), coarse structures (volumetric shapes based in the floor plan modules), a procedural decomposition method for subdividing features in those coarse structures (e.g. windows, doors, frames and others) and also a geometry factory to handle the representational purposes. The referred work preceded another system that produce buildings with complex facades, proposed by Finkenzeller and Schmitt [49]. In this system, designers must provide high-level requirements such as building coarse, type and style to produce highly accurate 3D buildings. They can also change facades parameters after building's generation, as the system is prepared for recomputing such modifications. A more mature version of this later system was presented by Finkenzeller [50] and it was used to produce the virtual model of the University of Karlsruhe. The realism of the exposed models is impressive. However, such level of detail requires spending between few minutes to about two hours per model, accordingly with the author.

2.2.6 Computer Generated Architecture for Buildings Production

Computer generated architecture (CGA) is another methodology related with outer facades generation, which relies on a rule system provided by shape grammars [3]. The process initiates with the creation of a mass model that constitutes the exterior format of a building, including the roof. This mass model can be seen as a merge of volumetric shapes that can variate in scale, rotation and usage portion. In the next step, facades are created to properly cover the mass models. The final step of the process increases the detail in doors and windows and also accommodates building ornaments. The grammar used in this technique—an extension of the split grammar— is sequential (similar to the Chomsky grammars addressed by Sipser [51]) and enables a large-scale production of buildings with different styles. A suburbia model of Beverly Hills was produced and depicted along with a procedural reconstruction of Pompeii, generated with 190 manually encoded CGA shape rules.

CGA was also applied in some works aiming virtual reconstructions [52–55]. Müller et al. [52] used it with the purpose of reconstructing Puuc-style buildings, that are similar structures to the ones found in Xkipché, México. In their work, the authors created a grammar to fulfil the architectonic requirements of the referred buildings. Thus, accordingly with the typical design of these structures, the grammar defines the building as following: first, the base is defined; then, middle walls are addressed considering building accesses; upon these walls, a middle-layer designated by medial moulding is produced; the last rules define frieze, cornice moulding and completion ornaments.

The same methodology was also applied by Dylla et al. [53] who produced a 3D reconstruction of ancient Rome (Fig. 2.2) through the combination of manually designed structures and procedurally generated buildings, in the same virtual environment. The class of each element defines what kind of approach is needed. For known positions, dimensions and design, class I elements are loaded from models created using a commercial computer aided design (CAD) software. If some information is missing, class II elements are generated procedurally using CGA shape methodology.

Besuievsky and Patow [54] developed their own CGA shape rules to reconstruct historic buildings and urban environments for serious games. They use as input 2D data provided by GIS with corrective mechanisms to deal with map issues, like distortion. This input allows the acquisition of relevant features such as building outlines, for further extrusions, forming mass models. The production of building facades is made through a user-friendly tool which hides the grammar to improve the easiness of use. The application of this methodology produced some interesting results on the virtual reconstruction of Carcassone's old town, in France. The tool's flexibility was demonstrated through the virtual reconstruction of two other cities with different architectonic styles: Nantes of France and Girona of Spain.

Tepavčević and Stojaković [55] combined developed a reliable mathematical model that combines fuzzy logic and probabilistic calculations to produce stochastic

Fig. 2.2 Virtual
reconstruction of ancient
Rome made by Dylla et al.
[53], using class I models
that were manually produced
and also class II models,
procedurally generated with
a CGA shape rules set in
order to overcome the lack of
information

Fig. 2.2 Virtual
reconstruction of ancient
Rome made by Dylla et al.
[53], using class I models
that were manually produced
and also class II models,
procedurally generated with
a CGA shape rules set in
order to overcome the lack of
information

CGA shape rules, that are used to generate realistic Neo-Gothic chapels. Each set
of rules defining a chapel starts by specifying a building lot and a mass model. The
mass model is decomposed in three main parts: apse, nave and tower. Apse and tower
mass model parts are replaced with appropriate shapes and the subsequent steps will
detail the model until the final 3D form.

2.2.7 Building Generation Based on Facade View Acquisition

A work focusing the decomposition of building facades through image analysis and
shape grammars was proposed by Müller et al. [56]. Their system starts by processing
a facade image and extracting its elements using automatic operations, through a
top–down hierarchical process. For example, a given facade image is divided into
floors which are, in turn, subdivided into tiles that are then partitioned into smaller
rectangles. Afterwards, a stage that consists in matching the last rectangles with a
library of 3D architectural elements, takes place. The whole process results in a tree
shape that is encoded into a shape grammar, which holds the definition for facade
representation.

A similar research line was followed by Koutsourakis et al. [57], who proposed a
framework capable of producing 3D models from a single facade image. Its inputs
are a parametric shape grammar and a rectified image of a single building facade. A
tree-based process takes over the generation, collecting a set of rules that regulate it
and, then, a Markov Random Field (MRF) formulation optimizes the parametric rules
to produce the buildings' final aspect. Later, Simon et al. [58] developed a system
that uses shape grammars and facade image classifiers to generate 3D buildings.
A combination of procedural modelling, statistics and image processing led to their
solution. Both of the previously referred works are extensively addressed on Simon's
Ph.D. thesis [59].

2.2.8   Digital Map-Based Generation of 3D Buildings with Multiple Roofs

Sugihara and Hayashi [60] proposed an automatic solution focused on the production of virtual buildings with multiple roofs, considering building footprints provided by digital maps. Using a system to express polygon angles and sort vertices (clockwise), their method is capable of splitting a building footprint into rectangles, that are used to determine roof branches and constitute the base shape for roof creation. The presented results demonstrate a set of buildings automatically generated, each one holding a set of gable roofs unified by branches. Moreover, complex roofs were also produced in order to fulfil the requirements for the reconstruction of an ancient japanese temple and also a pagoda.

2.2.9   City Modelling Procedural Engine (CMPE)

Carrozzino et al. [4] developed an engine that uses a set of input elements such as aerial photographs, vector and raster maps or even text descriptions, to produce extensive urban environments. At the beginning, streets data and block footprints are automatically extracted from the input maps. Then, a 2D road network is produced, followed by its 3D representation. 3D blocks and related buildings are subsequently generated. The buildings are produced considering user specifications or pseudo-random definitions. Further manual interventions for the refinement of the virtual buildings in post-production are also supported. A clean visualization of the whole scene is provided through the XVR rendering engine, incorporated in the CMPE.

2.2.10   Procedural Generation 3D (PG3D) Solution

A solution for procedural generation of extensive urban environments was presented by Silva and Coelho [5]. They opted by a strategy that consists in storing the instructions for modelling urban elements and geographic data in the same spatial database. The instructions for buildings' modelling are stored in database native language, pointing to the shape grammar rules. Each set of these rules can be seen as instructions to guide the geometric generation process of elements such as buildings, roofs or balconies. The presented results include the digital reproduction of some locals of Porto city (Portugal) with a considerable degree of resemblance (see Fig. 2.3). The extended version of this work can be found in the master thesis of Silva [61].

Fig. 2.3 Boavista roundabout produced by PG3D [5]. An available set of information was considered to generate the virtual model of this urban area, that has considerable degree of resemblance

2.2.11 Ontology-Based Generation of Urban Environments and Building Exteriors

The generation of ontology-based virtual urban environments was an area that few explored. In the current subsection, these works will be addressed.

2.2.11.1 Ontology-Based Procedural Modelling to Recover Cultural Heritage

An ontology-based solution was proposed by Liu et al. [11]. The authors embraced the challenge of recovering the cultural heritage of ancient China. To accomplish such challenge, a city generator was developed, capable of producing virtual models based on an ontology and on user input: a grammar for building definitions. Moreover, a style checker was implemented to avoid generation inconsistencies, such as buildings upon streets. Their work is also one of the few cases of an extensible ontology application that covers other architectonic styles. This system followed their previous work [10] in which a semantic-based modelling system was proposed. The objective was to improve users' focus on its specific implementation, while the geometric details are encapsulated by the semantic elements such as walls, doors and windows. In short, a user propagates the semantic information of a building using a XML format and then a document type definition verifies the XML conformity. Finally, in case of success a procedural modeller produces the geometry according with a user demands.

Recent works [37, 38] include some additional features. Yong et al. [37] reported the improvements made to the previous semantic-based solution [10] that intended to overcome some noted issues regarding procedural modelling, such as the lack of annotations for digital architectural heritage which also impacts in the identification of procedural rules for digital reconstruction of missing monuments. Such issues triggered the proposal of an approach that puts together semantics, machine intelligence, data mining and automatic annotations. Later, a granular ontology approach was suggested by Liu et al. [38] to allow a collaborative ontology design based on the sub-concepts provided by users of different expertise areas.

2.2.11.2   Semi-automatic Generation of Ontology-Based Building Facades

Bellotti et al. [39] proposed a statistical algorithm for the procedural generation of urban areas, capable of producing virtual buildings composed by several ontology-based facade components, considering georeferenced layouts and template styles statistically selected. The referred ontology is used to organize and relate several architectonic elements of facades such as windows, doors or roofs. The authors used the algorithm for the generation of urban environments in the context of cultural heritage promotion and in a 3D movie. Both were presented to users who rate positively the reconstruction, despite the absence of architectonic details, provided by elements like balconies or porches.

2.3   Procedural Modelling of Virtual Traversable Buildings

Besides the focus on urban environments and buildings outer facades, several other approaches address the procedural modelling of 3D traversable buildings. In the next subsections, they will be reviewed.

2.3.1   LaHave House: An Automated Architectural Design Service

Rau-Chaplin et al. [62] developed an automated architectural service to provide a collaborative way of plan and design modern houses, foreseeing the interaction between architects and final users (clients or service consumers). A design engine (that generates over 100,000 different house designs), a customization component (for the final user) and a building configuration tool are the three main components of this architectural service endowed with some automatic capabilities to process house designs.

2.3.2   Procedural Generation of Buildings Using Graphs and Expansion Algorithms

Martin [63] presented a procedural algorithm to generate residential units. Considering a grammar and user-defined constraints, the process starts by generating a graph

Fig. 2.4 An house with interiors produced by Martin's approach [64]: first, a graph system is used to connect and place rooms and then those rooms are increased in a fixed area using a Monte Carlo algorithm

in which nodes represent rooms and edges represent the connections between rooms. Then, those rooms are distributed within a footprint and, finally, a Monte Carlo algorithm expands them until equilibrium is reached. Figure 2.4 depicts the result of the author's approach. In his thesis, Martin [64] discusses graph-based techniques to generate structures of connected rooms and to place them within a given area. The process of room expansion is also explained in detail. Regardless of the similarities with the Monte Carlo algorithm, it seems that this designation was replaced by square bubble growing algorithm.

A similar solution—based on seed and growth approach—was proposed by Long [65]. This system considers as input an area for feature placement that can be rectangular or non-rectangular. Still, it is confined to shapes formed exclusively by right angles. The process of area fill includes the determination of feature types (shape variety) and also their placement and adjustment in the available space. The author argues that his technique is more effective than squarified treemaps approach (addressed in a later subsection).

2.3.3 Building Indoors Generation Using Constructive Solid Geometry Algorithms

Bradley [66] proposed a semi-automatic methodology to produce traversable buildings which considers two types of input: American Standard Code for Information Interchange (ASCII) files with heuristics and room definitions and building outline. Some 2D and 3D Constructive Solid Geometry (CSG) algorithms are used to deal with division of the building outline into rectangular cells, walls extrusion, placement of door and windows, among other operations. The outputs results are 3D traversable buildings devoid of any details.

2.3.4   Lazy Production of Virtual Building Interiors

The concept of real-time generation of interior divisions was exploited by Hahn et al. [6]. The plans of each floor are generated through a random division of the floor into rectangular divisions and hall passages. The division process starts by defining a temporary region which is then divided in smaller temporary regions and built regions. This is repeated iteratively until each region becomes a built region. The authors also implemented some architectonic rules to ensure the proper generation of the final geometry.

2.3.5   Interior Rooms Generated Through Voronoi Diagrams and Constrained by Convex Layouts

Dahl and Rinde [67] developed an algorithm that generates rooms inside polygons representing building limits (Fig. 2.5). It receives a set of specifications for building generation such as constraint walls, windows and doors and also a couple of parameters defining region types and room types. Then, it mounts the building skeleton with a mandatory corridor for layouts with large dimensions and creates regions for grouping sub-regions or final rooms. These last elements are generated using a weighted Voronoi diagram that spreads rooms inside regions considering the desired room weights. Meanwhile, a room graph is created in order to connect rooms and then, the room types are defined accordingly with the input parameters.

This approach generates traversable buildings considering irregular shapes as constraints. However, some issues were identified: the impossibility of managing the number and size of rooms to be generated; the confinement to the generation of structures disregarding geometric holes; finally, the absence of visual details such as textures.

Fig. 2.5 Dahl and Rinde [67] used a Voronoi diagram to subdivide an irregular polygon into rooms

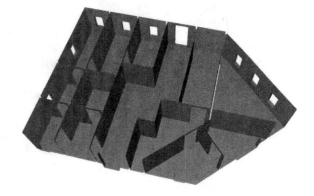

2.3.6 Rule-Based Generation/Reconstruction of Buildings

Rodrigues [68, 69] proposed a rule-based method capable of generating portuguese houses (regulated by [70]) and reconstructing ancient roman houses (regulated by Maciel [71]). Several steps such as room graph definition, floor plan composition using shapes and extrusions considering doors and windows lead to the 3D model achievement. Rodrigues et al. [72] revealed, in detail, the methods and processes carried out to generate roman houses, which include spontaneous L-systems, multi-layer graphs defining containers and also room connections, among other relevant procedural operations. Later, Rodrigues et al. [73] extended their work to provide virtual building models in several formats (for example, X3D and VRML). The improvement foresees the integration with virtual platforms like Second Life. The aforementioned works culminated on a doctoral thesis [74] that has some images depicting virtual reconstructions of roman houses like the ones that can be seen in Fig. 2.6.

2.3.7 Squarified Treemaps for Virtual Buildings Generation

The squarified treemap [75] is a subdivision strategy (Fig. 2.7) adapted for the generation of buildings with interiors. The strategy consists in splitting rectangular areas considering a set of weights and the following key rule: in each division it must be ensured that the aspect ratio has the closest value to 1. Marson and Musse [7] applied it to subdivide rectangular building footprints into functional zones and then rooms. The final step is the placement of a corridor to connect the unreachable rooms. Mirahmadi and Shami [76] used the same method with some optimizations at the corridor placement step, to increase the realism of the architectural designs.

Fig. 2.6 Virtual environment depicting roman houses [74]. A set of reconstruction rules is used to guide the cultural heritage recovering process from the floor plan stage to the complete 3D building model

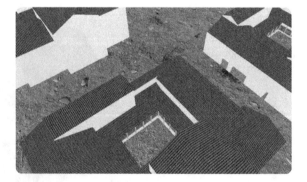

Fig. 2.7 Squarified treemaps operation [75]. Considering the following sequence of rectangular areas 6, 6, 4, 3, 2, 2 and 1, a descendant sorting algorithm optimizes the process which tries to arrange the areas inside a rectangular container, in order to find the aspect ratio with the closest value to 1, in each iteration

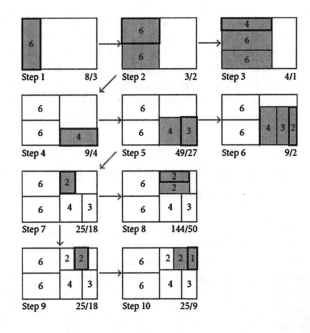

2.3.8 Residential Buildings Generation Based on Bayesian Networks

An approach for generating virtual models of residential buildings, focusing the production of floor plans highly based on architectonic knowledge, was presented by Merrell et al. [8]. In this approach, a set of high-level requirements must be provided by an user and then expanded into an architectural program, that consists in a bubble diagram providing a list of rooms, respective sizes and connections. The architectural program—compatible with the referred requirements—is provided by a bayesian network that contains 120 of these structures manually encoded. Next, the floor plan is determined through stochastic optimization that occurs using operations such as wall sliding and room swapping. Afterwards, the 3D model generation takes place, considering a selected template that aims to garnish the building with an appearance style.

2.3.9 Grid Approach Focusing Floor Plan Generation

A method inspired in geometric grids used by architects to aid the manual drawing of floor plans was proposed by Lopes et al. [77], who developed a grid-based algorithm to allow the placement and expansion of rooms. Taking into consideration a few user inputs (for example grid size, list of room, respective types and dimension), first, the functional zones are determined (e.g. public and private zones) as it was also suggested by Marson and Musse [7]. Then, rooms are placed in the proper zones and expanded using the grid approach. The placement step defines the appropriated position of a room in the grid. Then, growth methods based on cells filling are applied to make the rooms expand through the available area. At last, the connections are processed accordingly with connectivity requirements or definition rules to complete the floor plan.

2.3.10 Generative Modelling Language (GML) for Virtual Buildings

GML—acronym for generative modelling language in the specific context of this work (different from Geographic Modelling Language)—is an imperative programming language used to define geometric structures based on split grammars [78], that also supports the generation of building interiors. The available operations include the creation, modification and termination of scopes and also relative and absolute subdivisions. The tool effectiveness was demonstrated through a case study that consisted in the reconstruction of the University of Technology in Graz, Austria, which involved several steps ranging from the identification of superstructures (subparts of the same building) till the linkage of floors using staircases. More information about this language can be found in [79].

2.3.11 Component-Based Modelling of Virtual Buildings

Leblanc et al. [80] proposed a tool that requires programming skills to support the component-oriented modelling of virtual buildings. Each component can be seen as a geometric element of the building (2D or 3D shape), composed by faces or regions. The referred programming tool allows some operations upon components such as attribute alteration (add, modify or delete), component connection (consists on linking a component coordinates system to another component region) or creation (that includes, for example, instantiating, slicing, splitting, extruding or roofing components for geometric transformations or decomposition). Despite the high-level of freedom, a sequence of steps is suggested towards the attainment of the expected virtual models: space partitioning into roofs, storeys and rooms; extrusion of interiors and exteriors; placement of architectural elements such as windows, doors and balconies; and placement of furniture.

2.3.12 Producing Virtual 3D Buildings from Pre-designed Floor Plans

A tool for the expeditious production of 3D virtual buildings, including interiors and outer facades, considering scanned floor plans among other input information such as photos, room areas, location and surroundings was proposed by Santos et al. [81]. At a preparatory stage, some user inputs have to be provided in order to accomplish a few operations such as the floor plan vectorization through digital decal drawings and the indication of staircases. Subsequently, the entire geometry providing 3D visualization is produced considering the following steps: wall extrusion, placement of doors and windows, inclusion of interior furniture and, finally, roofs creation. Furthermore, some virtual elements are generated out-of-doors to integrate the building surroundings. Other interesting features that worth to highlight are, for example, the rule-based furniture placement, the realistic texturing and the (manual or automatic) creation of virtual visitations.

The prototype Building Model Generator (BMG) was another proposal that appeared even earlier than the previously mentioned [82]. The prototype receives as input 2D floor plans, previously developed in a commercial CAD software. Then, the floor plans are properly converted to a compatible BMG format and the prototype posteriorly detects and corrects small geometrical inconsistencies. Those floor plans are analyzed in order to extract rooms and portals. Further steps include the extrusion of walls and also the proper placement of doors and windows. An interactive editor is provided to allow some adjustments on building elements, including materials. Finally, there is a complementary tool—a staircase generator—that enables the proper placement of staircases. The final result is a virtual 3D model of a building with connected floors.

2.3.13 Ontology-Based Generation of Traversable Buildings

The ontology-based modelling of traversable buildings was also addressed by a few authors. The current subsection will expose each work.

2.3.13.1 Virtual World Grammar for Automatic Generation of Virtual Worlds

An ontology-based virtual world (VW) generator focusing institutions was proposed by Trescak et al. [9]. The case study provided by the authors is an auction system, represented by a set of activities: admission, item registration, auction, auction info and also entrances and exits. Then, a VW Grammar is constructed, based on an ontology. The referred ontology comprises both activities and a shape grammar. An object mapping is also performed in order to relate ontological objects with the proper shape grammar responsible for its representation in the virtual world. After the completion of VW Grammar, a set of heuristics, validations and evaluations regulate the generation of the institution, that is made in two main steps: floor plan production and 3D virtual model transformation.

2.3.13.2   Framework of Procedural Techniques

Tutenel et al. [83] proposed an inclusive framework that produces virtual buildings using several procedural techniques. Building floor plan definitions must be provided using declarative language instructions, that trigger a sequence of steps including the loading of the floor plans and the selection of the techniques that should be used in each phase of generation. For example, lot (3D building gross model) generation can be made through CGA shape grammar and the floor plan might be produced using a grid approach like the one presented by Lopes et al. [77]. Some regulation mechanisms are applied to guide the whole process aiming, for example, the assignment of a convenient procedural technique for each building element to be generated and the avoidance of functional conflicts (bad placement of objects, such as regular room windows in bathrooms).

2.4   Summary

This chapter started by presenting the versatility of ontologies applied in a wide variety of solutions incorporating, 3D virtual models to serve areas such as medicine, industry, cultural heritage and design. Then, standard knowledge-based representations for virtual urban environments were addressed: CityGML was referred and shown along with the building definition proposed by this standard. Moreover, the procedural modelling solutions were extensively documented, including the generation/reconstruction of virtual urban environments and traversable buildings. Each topic had a few works that also consider ontologies.

Summing up, there is a wide variety of procedural modelling works addressing the generation of virtual buildings' interiors with distinct approaches: tools based on shape grammars [62], CSG algorithms [66], expanding rooms [64], grid-based approaches [77], squarified treemaps [7, 76], rule-based solutions [74] with architectonic awareness [70, 71], generative modelling languages [78, 80] and others. However, most of them only deal with rectangular shapes or geometries uniquely formed by right angles. Alternatively, Dahl and Rinde [67] addressed the production of virtual buildings composed by convex shapes with a Voronoi diagram approach. However, some issues remain to be addressed, including: (1) the lack of support to holes in the middle of floor plans; (2) the apparent inappropriateness of the rooms' generation approach when the control over rooms' features (such as geometric constraints and arrangements) is required; and (3) the absence of textures that hamper the visual distinction of, for example, room types.

Considering the referred issues, a novel procedural modelling methodology will be presented along with a building ontology—for regulation purposes—inspired in the exposed ontology works and in the CityGML standard. The referred methodology contains a process that relies in some of the aforementioned procedural modelling solutions, specifically in the floor plan generation and the 3D transformation. The refinements made during the development of this methodology will be progressively presented until the final solution, that supports the generation of buildings constrained by arbitrary shapes, with rooms limited by a configurable number of inner walls. This solution also intends to enable the generation of virtual buildings in different architectural contexts, taking advantage from the integrated building ontology. General purpose buildings belonging to the generic ontology, T2 houses complying with portuguese architectural rules and buildings based on roman architecture—specifically *domus*—are addressed as case studies and for demonstration purposes. Moreover, a stochastic approach regarding the random generation of virtual generic buildings will be presented as a way of automating the virtual models production using this methodology.

References

 1. Parish, Y.I.H., Müller, P.: Procedural modeling of cities. In: Proceedings of the 28th Annual Conference on Computer Graphics and Interactive Techniques, SIGGRAPH '01, pp. 301–308, New York, NY, USA, 2001. ACM (2001). ISBN 1-58113-374-X. doi:10.1145/383259.383292
 2. Wonka, P., Wimmer, M., Sillion, F., Ribarsky, W.: Instant architecture. ACM Trans. Graph. **22**(3), 669–677 (2003). ISSN 0730-0301. doi:10.1145/882262.882324
 3. Müller, P., Wonka, P., Haegler, S., Ulmer, A., Van Gool, L.: Procedural modeling of buildings. ACM Trans. Graph. **25**(3), 614–623 (2006). ISSN 0730-0301. doi:10.1145/1141911.1141931
 4. Carrozzino, M., Tecchia, F., Bergamasco, M.: Urban procedural modeling for real-time rendering. In: Proceedings of the 3rd ISPRS International Workshop 3D-ARCH, vol. 2009 (2009)
 5. Silva, P.B., Coelho, A.: Procedural modeling for realistic virtual worlds development. J. Virtual Worlds Res. **4**(1) (2011). doi:10.4101/jvwr.v4i1.2109. https://journals.tdl.org/jvwr/index.php/jvwr/article/view/2109/5541
 6. Hahn, E., Bose, P., Whitehead, A.: Lazy generation of building interiors in realtime. In: Canadian Conference on Electrical and Computer Engineering, 2006. CCECE '06, pp. 2441–2444, May 2006. doi:10.1109/CCECE.2006.277767
 7. Marson, F., Raupp Musse, S.: Automatic real-time generation of floor plans based on squarified treemaps algorithm. Int. J. Comput. Games Technol. **2010**, 7:1–7:10 (2010). ISSN 1687-7047. doi:10.1155/2010/624817
 8. Merrell, P., Schkufza, E., Koltun, V.: Computer-generated residential building layouts. ACM Trans. Graph. **29**(6), 181:1–181:12 (2010). ISSN 0730-0301. doi:10.1145/1882261.1866203
 9. Trescak, T., Esteva, M., Rodriguez, I.: A virtual world grammar for automatic generation of virtual worlds. Vis. Comput. **26**(6-8), 521–531 (2010). ISSN 0178-2789. doi:10.1007/s00371-010-0473-7
10. Liu, Y., Xu, C., Pan, Z., Pan, Y.: Semantic modeling for ancient architecture of digital heritage. Comput. Graph. **30**(5), 800–814 (2006). ISSN 0097-8493. doi:10.1016/j.cag.2006.07.008. http://www.sciencedirect.com/science/article/pii/S0097849306001294
11. Liu, Y., Xu, C., Zhang, Q., Pan, Y.: The smart architect: scalable ontology-based modeling of ancient chinese architectures. IEEE Intell. Syst. **23**(1), 49–56 (2008). ISSN 1541-1672

12. Borgo, S., Guarino, N., Masolo, C.: An ontological theory of physical objects. In: Proceedings of Qualitative Reasoning 11th International Workshop, pp. 223–231 (1997)
13. Noy, N.F., Hafner, C.D.: The state of the art in ontology design: a survey and comparative review. AI Mag. **18**(3), 53 (1997)
14. Richard Benjamins, V., Fensel, D.: The ontological engineering initiative (ka)2 (1998)
15. Wand, Y., Weber, R.: An ontological model of an information system. IEEE Trans. Softw. Eng. **16**(11), 1282–1292 (1990)
16. Weber, R., Coopers & Lybrand: Ontological Foundations of Information Systems. Coopers & Lybrand accounting research methodology monograph. Coopers & Lybrand and the Accounting Association of Australia and New Zealand (1997)
17. van Heijst, G., Schreiber, A.Th., Wielinga, B.J.: Using explicit ontologies in kbs development. Int. J. Hum.-Comput. Stud. **46**(2), 183–292 (1997). ISSN 1071-5819. doi:10.1006/ijhc.1996.0090. http://www.sciencedirect.com/science/article/pii/S1071581996900907
18. Guarino, N.: Formal ontology and information systems. In: Proceedings of the First International Conference (FOIS'98), pp. 3–15. IOS Press (1998)
19. Chandrasekaran, B., Josephson, J.R., Benjamins, V.R.: What are ontologies, and why do we need them? IEEE Intell. Syst. Appl. **14**(1), 20–26 (1999). ISSN 1094-7167. doi:10.1109/5254.747902
20. Jannin, P., Morandi, X.: Surgical models for computer-assisted neurosurgery. Neuroimage **37**(3), 783–791 (2007)
21. Attene, M., Robbiano, F., Spagnuolo, M., Falcidieno, B.: Characterization of 3d shape parts for semantic annotation. Comput.-Aided Des. **41**(10), 756–763 (2009)
22. Béhé, F., Galland, S., Gaud, N., Nicolle, C., Koukam, A.: An ontology-based metamodel for multiagent-based simulations. Simul. Modell. Pract. Theory **40**(0), 64–85 (2014). ISSN 1569-190X. doi:10.1016/j.simpat.2013.09.002. http://www.sciencedirect.com/science/article/pii/S1569190X13001342
23. Pittarello, F., De Faveri, A.: Semantic description of 3d environments: a proposal based on web standards. In: Proceedings of the Eleventh International Conference on 3D Web Technology, pp. 85–95. ACM (2006)
24. García-Rojas, A., Gutiérrez, M., Thalmann, D.: Visual creation of inhabited 3d environments. Vis. Comput. **24**(7–9), 719–726 (2008)
25. Lee, J.Y., Seo, D.W., Rhee, G.: Visualization and interaction of pervasive services using context-aware augmented reality. Expert Syst. Appl. **35**(4), 1873–1882 (2008). ISSN 0957-4174. doi:10.1016/j.eswa.2007.08.092. http://www.sciencedirect.com/science/article/pii/S0957417407003818
26. Hunter, J., Gerber, A.: Harvesting community annotations on 3d models of museum artefacts to enhance knowledge, discovery and re-use. J. Cult. Herit. **11**(1), 81–90 (2010)
27. Martins TMP: Ontologia urbana para ambiente virtual colaborativo no contexto do planeamento e gestao municipais. Master's thesis, Faculdade de Engenharia da Universidade do Porto (2011)
28. Colledani, M., Pedrielli, G., Terkaj, W., Urgo, M.: Integrated virtual platform for manufacturing systems design. Proc. CIRP **7**, 425–430 (2013)
29. Flotynski, J.: Semantic modelling of interactive 3d content with domain-specific ontologies. Proc. Comput. Sci. **35**(0), 531–540 (2014). ISSN 1877-0509. doi:10.1016/j.procs.2014.08.134. http://www.sciencedirect.com/science/article/pii/S1877050914010990. In: Proceedings of the Knowledge-Based and Intelligent Information & Engineering Systems 18th Annual Conference, KES-2014 Gdynia, Poland, September 2014
30. Mignard, C., Nicolle, C.: Merging bim and gis using ontologies application to urban facility management in active3d. Comput. Ind. **65**(9), 1276–1290 (2014). ISSN 0166-3615. doi:10.1016/j.compind.2014.07.008. http://www.sciencedirect.com/science/article/pii/S0166361514001432. Special Issue on The Role of Ontologies in Future Web-based Industrial Enterprises
31. Galambos, P., Csapó, Á., Zentay, P., Fülöp, I.M., Haidegger, T., Baranyi, P., Rudas, I.J.: Design, programming and orchestration of heterogeneous manufacturing systems through vr-powered remote collaboration. Robot. Comput.-Integr. Manuf. (2014). ISSN 0736-5845. doi:10.1016/j.rcim.2014.08.012. http://www.sciencedirect.com/science/article/pii/S0736584514000738

32. Gröger, G., Kolbe, T.H., Czerwinski, A., Nagel, C.: OGC City Geography Markup Language (CityGML) Encoding Standard. Technical report, Open Geospatial Consortium (2008)
33. Gröger, G., Kolbe, T.H., Nagel, C., Häfele, K.-H.: OGC City Geography Markup Language (CityGML) Encoding Standard. Technical report, Open Geospatial Consortium (2012)
34. Kolbe, T.H.: Representing and exchanging 3d city models with citygml. In: 3D Geo-information Sciences, pp. 15–31. Springer (2009)
35. Liebich, T.: Ifc4–the new buildingsmart standard (2013)
36. BuildingSMART: Industry foundation classes release 4. http://www.buildingsmart-tech.org/ifc/IFC4/final/html/ (2013). Accessed May 2015
37. Yong, L., Mingmin, Z., Yunliang, J., Haiying, Z.: Improving procedural modeling with semantics in digital architectural heritage. Comput. Graph. **36**(3), 178–184 (2012). ISSN 0097-8493. doi:10.1016/j.cag.2012.01.003. http://www.sciencedirect.com/science/article/pii/S0097849312000040. Novel Applications of VR
38. Liu, Y., Zheng, X., Tang, F., Chen, X.: Ontology design with a granular approach. Expert Syst. Appl. **41**(10), 4867–4877 (2014). ISSN 0957-4174. doi:10.1016/j.eswa.2014.02.019. http://www.sciencedirect.com/science/article/pii/S0957417414000827
39. Bellotti, F., Berta, R., Cardona, R., De Gloria, A.: An architectural approach to efficient 3d urban modeling. Comput. Graph. **35**(5), 1001–1012 (2011)
40. Lindenmayer, A.: Mathematical models for cellular interactions in development ii. simple and branching filaments with two-sided inputs. J. Theor. Biol. **18**(3), 300–315 (1968). ISSN 0022-5193. doi:10.1016/0022-5193(68)90080-5. http://www.sciencedirect.com/science/article/pii/0022519368900805
41. Coelho, A., Bessa, M., Augusto Sousa, A., Nunes Ferreira, F.: Expeditious modelling of virtual urban environments with geospatial l-systems. In: Computer Graphics Forum, vol. 26, pp. 769–782. Wiley Online Library (2007)
42. Larive, M., Gaildrat, V.: Wall grammar for building generation. In: Proceedings of the 4th International Conference on Computer Graphics and Interactive Techniques in Australasia and Southeast Asia, GRAPHITE '06, pp. 429–437, New York, NY, USA, 2006. ACM (2006). ISBN 1-59593-564-9. doi:10.1145/1174429.1174501
43. Felkel, P., Obdrzalek, S.: Straight skeleton implementation. In: Proceedings of Spring Conference on Computer Graphics (1998)
44. Eppstein, D., Erickson, J.: Raising roofs, crashing cycles, and playing pool: applications of a data structure for finding pairwise interactions. In: Proceedings of the Fourteenth Annual Symposium on Computational Geometry, SCG '98, pp. 58–67, New York, NY, USA, 1998. ACM (1998). ISBN 0-89791-973-4. doi:10.1145/276884.276891
45. Dikaiakou, M., Efthymiou, A., Chrysanthou, Y.: Modelling the walled city of nicosia. In: Proceedings of the 4th International Conference on Virtual Reality, Archaeology and Intelligent Cultural Heritage, VAST'03, pp. 61–70, Aire-la-Ville, Switzerland, Switzerland, 2003. Eurographics Association (2003). ISBN 3-905673-08-8. doi:10.2312/VAST/VAST03/061-070
46. Aichholzer, O., Aurenhammer, F.: Straight Skeletons for General Polygonal Figures in the Plane, pp. 117–126. Springer (1996)
47. Greuter, S., Parker, J., Stewart, N., Leach, G.: Real-time procedural generation of 'pseudo infinite' cities. In: Proceedings of the 1st International Conference on Computer Graphics and Interactive Techniques in Australasia and South East Asia, GRAPHITE '03, pp. 87–ff, New York, NY, USA, 2003. ACM (2003). ISBN 1-58113-578-5. doi:10.1145/604471.604490
48. Finkenzeller, D., Bender, J., Schmitt, A.: Feature-based decomposition of facades. In: Proceedings of the Virtual Concept (2005)
49. Finkenzeller, D., Schmitt, A.: Rapid modeling of complex building façades. Institut für Betriebs-und Dialogsysteme, Universität Karlsruhe (TH), Germany (2006)
50. Finkenzeller, D.: Detailed building facades. IEEE Comput. Graph. Appl. **28**(3), 58–66 (2008). ISSN 0272-1716. doi:10.1109/MCG.2008.50
51. Sipser, M.: Introduction to the Theory of Computation. Course Technology, Boston (1996)
52. Müller, P., Vereenooghe, T., Wonka, P., Paap, I., Van Gool, L.: Procedural 3d reconstruction of puuc buildings in xkipché. In: Eurographics Symposium on Virtual Reality, Archaeology and Cultural Heritage (VAST), pp. 139–146. EG (2006)

53. Dylla, K., Muller, P., Ulmer, A., Haegler, S., Fischer, B.: Rome reborn 2.0: a case study of virtual city reconstruction using procedural modeling techniques. In: Proceedings of Computer Applications and Quantitative Methods in Archaeology (2009)
54. Besuievsky, G., Patow, G.: Procedural modeling historical buildings for serious games. Virtual Archaeol. Rev. 4(9), 160–166 (2013). ISSN 1989-9947. http://varjournal.es/doc/varj04_009_23.pdf
55. Tepavčević, B., Stojaković, V.: Procedural modeling in architecture based on statistical and fuzzy inference. Autom. Constr. 35(0), 329–337 (2013). ISSN 0926-5805. doi:10.1016/j.autcon.2013.05.015. http://www.sciencedirect.com/science/article/pii/S0926580513000824
56. Müller, P., Zeng, G., Wonka, P., Van Gool L.: Image-based procedural modeling of facades. In: ACM Transactions on Graphics (TOG), vol. 26, p. 85. ACM (2007)
57. Koutsourakis, P., Simon, L., Teboul, O., Tziritas, G., Paragios, N.: Single view reconstruction using shape grammars for urban environments. In: 2009 IEEE 12th International Conference on Computer Vision, pp. 1795–1802. IEEE (2009)
58. Simon, L., Teboul, O., Koutsourakis, P., Paragios, N.: Random exploration of the procedural space for single-view 3d modeling of buildings. Int. J. Comput. Vis. 93(2), 253–271 (2011)
59. Simon, L.: Procedural reconstruction of buildings: towards large scale automatic 3D modeling of urban environments. Theses, Ecole Centrale Paris, July 2011. https://tel.archives-ouvertes.fr/tel-00637638
60. Sugihara, K., Hayashi, Y.: Automatic generation of 3d building models with multiple roofs. Tsinghua Sci. Technol. 13, 368–374 (2008)
61. Silva, P.B.: Modelacao procedimental para desenvolvimento de jogos de computador. Master's thesis, Faculdade de Engenharia da Universidade do Porto (2010)
62. Rau-Chaplin, A., MacKay-Lyons, B., Spierenburg, P.: The lahave house project: towards and automated architectural design service. In: Proceedings of the International Conference on Computer Aided Design (CADEX-96), pp. 62–66. IEEE (1996)
63. Martin, J.: Algorithmic beauty of buildings methods for procedural building generation. Computer Science Honors Theses, p. 4 (2005)
64. Martin, J.: Procedural house generation: a method for dynamically generating floor plans. In: Symposium on Interactive 3D Graphics and Games (2006)
65. Long, J.H.: Room and feature placement for procedurally generated indoor environments. Ph.D. thesis, University of Abertay Dundee (2011)
66. Bradley, B.: Towards the procedural generation of urban building interiors. Ph.D. thesis, M.Sc. thesis, Game Programming, University of Hull (2005)
67. Dahl, A., Rinde, L.: Procedural generation of indoor environments. Master Thesis with shared authorship, Charmers University of Technology (2008)
68. Rodrigues, N., Dionísio, M., Gonçalves, A., Magalhães, L.M.G., Moura, J.P.: Rule-based generation of houses. Comput. Graph. Geom. 10(2), 49–65 (2008). http://cgg-journal.com/2008-2/05/index.html
69. Rodrigues, N., Dionísio, M., Gonçalves, A., Magalhães, L.G., Moura, J.P., Chalmers, A.: Incorporating legal rules on procedural house generation. In: Proceedings of the 24th Spring Conference on Computer Graphics, SCCG '08, pp. 59–66, New York, NY, USA, 2008. ACM (2008). ISBN 978-1-60558-957-2. doi:10.1145/1921264.1921279
70. RGEU: Regulamento geral das edificações urbanas, decreto n. ° 38382 (2008)
71. Maciel, M.: Vitrúvio - Tratado De Arquitetura. Ist Press (2006)
72. Rodrigues, N., Gonzaga Magalhães, L., Paulo Moura, J., Chalmers, A.: Automatic reconstruction of virtual heritage sites. In: Proceedings of the 9th International conference on Virtual Reality, Archaeology and Cultural Heritage, pp. 39–46. Eurographics Association (2008)
73. Rodrigues, N., Magalhães, L., Moura, J., Chalmers, A., Santos, F., Morgado, L.: Archhousegenerator—a framework for house generation. J. Virtual Worlds Res. 2(5) (2010). ISSN 1941–8477. https://journals.tdl.org/jvwr/index.php/jvwr/article/view/846
74. Rodrigues, N.: Rule-based generation of virtual traversable architectural-period houses. Ph.D. thesis, University of Trás-os-Montes e Alto Douro (2010)

75. Bruls, M., Huizing, K., van Wijk, J.: Squarified treemaps. In: Proceedings of the Joint Euro-graphics and IEEE TCVG Symposium on Visualization, pp. 33–42. Press (1999)
76. Mirahmadi, M., Shami, A.: A novel algorithm for real-time procedural generation of building floor plans. CoRR, abs/1211.5842 (2012)
77. Lopes, R., Tim, T., Smelik, R.M., de Kraker, K.J., Bidarra, R.: A constrained growth method for procedural floor plan generation. In: GAMEON'10, November 2010. http://graphics.tudelft.nl/~rafa/myPapers/bidarra.GAMEON10.pdf
78. Hohmann, B., Havemann, S., Krispel, U., Fellner, D.: A GML shape grammar for semantically enriched 3d building models. Comput. Graph. **34**(4), 322–334 (2010). ISSN 0097-8493. doi:10.1016/j.cag.2010.05.007. http://www.sciencedirect.com/science/article/pii/S0097849310000749. Procedural Methods in Computer Graphics Illustrative Visualization
79. Havemann, S.: Generative Mesh Modeling. Ph.D. thesis (2005). http://deposit.ddb.de/cgi-bin/dokserv?idn=977813207
80. Leblanc, L., Houle, J., Poulin, P.: Component-based modeling of complete buildings. In: Pro-ceedings of Graphics Interface 2011, GI '11, pp. 87–94, School of Computer Science, Univer-sity of Waterloo, Waterloo, Ontario, Canada, 2011. Canadian Human-Computer Communica-tions Society. ISBN 978-1-4503-0693-5. http://dl.acm.org/citation.cfm?id=1992917.1992932
81. Santos, D.S.S., Dionísio, M., Rodrigues, N., Pereira, A.: Efficient creation of 3d models from buildings floor plans. Int. J. Interactive Worlds **2011**, 1–30 (2011). doi:10.5171/2011.897069
82. Lewis, R., Séquin. C.: Generation of 3d building models from 2d architectural plans. Comput.-Aided Des. **30**(10), 765–779 (1998). ISSN 0010-4485. doi:10.1016/S0010-4485(98)00031-1. http://www.sciencedirect.com/science/article/pii/S0010448598000311
83. Tutenel, T., Smelik, R.M., Lopes, R., de Kraker, K.J., Bidarra, R.: Generating consistent build-ings: a semantic approach for integrating procedural techniques. IEEE Trans. Comput. Intell. AI Games **3**(3), 274–288 (2011). ISSN 1943-068X. doi:10.1109/TCIAIG.2011.2162842

Chapter 3
Procedural Modelling Methodology Overview

Abstract This chapter provides an overview of the procedural modelling methodology that is addressed in this book. With the purpose of pointing out its need, the current issues in Procedural Modelling will be highlighted. In addition, the justification of some strategic decisions made during the development activities will be presented along with a brief enlightenment of the aforementioned methodology.

3.1 Problem Definition and General Proposed Framework

Regardless of the variety of approaches that can be found in the vast procedural modelling bibliography, techniques capable of joining traversable buildings and non-squared geometries in the same bundle are still scarce. Moreover, mechanisms regarding extensions to specific architectonic styles seem to be under-explored. The identification of such shortcomings triggered the definition of a new ontology-based methodology, capable of generating buildings constrained by arbitrary shapes and composed by inner rooms, that can also vary in terms of geometry.

At the beginning of this journey, the goal of producing different types of buildings with possibly diverse architectonic styles was pursued. Ontologies were then chosen to overcome the challenge, because for procedural modelling, ontologies may act as regulatory structures, that relate a building's conceptual parts with the geometrical aspects considering both as distinct objects. Moreover, they promote scalability and reusability, as it was demonstrated by Béhé et al. [1] and Mignard and Nicolle [2], providing useful extension mechanisms, as it commonly happens on information systems' data models. There was also some experience gathered in the combination of procedural modelling and ontologies, as it was previously explored, with success, in the Expedite Virtual Reconstruction of Cultural Heritage Sites (ERAS) research project,[1] in which a semi-automatic methodology was applied for the

---

[1]The project "Expedite Virtual Reconstruction of Cultural Heritage Sites" (ERAS—PTDC/EIA-EIA/114868/2009) aimed to create a tool for the field of archaeology which made it possible to rebuild and visualize georeferenced archaeological sites with complete buildings, indoors and outdoors.

© The Author(s) 2016

T. Adão et al., *Ontology-based Procedural Modelling of Traversable Buildings Composed by Arbitrary Shapes*, SpringerBriefs in Computer Science, DOI 10.1007/978-3-319-42372-2_3

virtual reconstruction of virtual buildings belonging to distinct epochs, using previously extracted rules from textual descriptions. The previously mentioned characteristics and advantages of ontologies, together with the experience acquired from the ERAS project, led to the planning and design of a generic ontology that can be extended to characterize different kinds of building in different architectural contexts. Regarding the new procedural modelling methodology that is about to be presented, the roman architectural style is the first case-study addressed mainly because there is a lot of accurate documentation available that can be used to support and validate some of the produced virtual models [3–6]. Simultaneously, the viability of adapting ontology extensions—to that methodology, aiming the generation of different structures was also being ascertained. These extensions are made from a generic ontology which was designed considering CityGML [7, 8]: a standard that can be seen as a set of recommendations for describing virtual urban environments.

The procedural modelling methodology was addressed soon after the ontology design phase. During the literature review, it became obvious that most of the existing procedural modelling methods for the generation of virtual buildings populated with inner rooms, starts by solving the floor plan production task. The identification of this pattern led to the first challenge: to find an adequate space division approach.

An extensive research took place and a wide variety of approaches was analysed. Most of them rely on the rectangular subdivision or aggregation of rectangular shapes. Rau-Chaplin et al. [9] created a shape grammar-based tool to allow the collaborative building plan and design between architects and clients. According to the authors, *tiles* are room's configurations related with furniture organization—among others— that suggest that rooms are confined to rectangular shapes: a guess reinforced by the floor plans depicted on their paper. Martin [10] proposed a Monte-Carlo expansion approach that makes the rooms growth and fill a given footprint. He confirmed that room's base shapes are also confined to rectangles as other works proposed by Lopes et al. [11], Rodrigues [12], Merrell et al. [13] or Tutenel et al. [14]. An alternative approach [15, 16], operating with same kinds of shapes, involve the floor plan subdivision with squarified treemaps [17]. This solution focus the space provisioning and considers a set of rectangles—sorted by weights of occupation—along with their aspect ratios to arrange rooms inside a given rectangular container. The goal is to fit this rectangles inside the container forcing them to have the closest possible aspect ratio from value 1, in each iteration. Such restrictive method is inappropriate to generate buildings in scenarios that require a certain level of controllability over the placement of rooms (for example, in tasks regarding building's reconstruction or digital preservation). The same issue affects the *lazy* approach of Hahn et al. [18] who proposed a rectangular subdivision of building floors based on random number generation, in real time. Others [19, 20] opted by generative modelling languages and CSG algorithms that require designers to have programming skills. Besides, virtual buildings' construction process seems to be quite tedious, despite the announced production time decreasing tendency, over the iterations with the tools. Only one work was found with the goal of dealing with non-rectangular shapes during the floor plan production: [21] in which a Voronoi-based method to subdivide randomly shaped rooms constrained by irregular polygons was developed. This work has, however, some drawbacks that include the impossibility of producing floor plans with geometric holes in the middle, the lack of control over rooms' features (such as number, geometry and size) and the absence of textures for the visual distinction of buildings' elements (as it was already explained in Chap. 2).

Alternatively, treemap [22] was identified as an effective space partition approach (specially when using recursion) simple to apply, highly controllable, predictable and quite flexible. Although this approach have been applied to the rectangular space partitioning, the resulting rectangles can be interpreted as bounding boxes defining room's shapes prone to modification through the insertion or removal of shape's edges that represent wall's segments. Thereby, treemap approach is the chosen candidate to integrate the procedural modelling methodology that is being presented in this book, specifically in the floor plan generation task.

The treemap approach was initially applied to generate roman houses—also known as *domus*—composed by rectangular divisions and rectangular layouts, as it will be seen in Chap. 4. Buildings with such room configurations are suitable for the use of this approach. Although the treemap approach is usually associated with squared shapes, this did not discourage its incorporation in the new procedural modelling methodology that is being presented. In fact, the treemap was successfully adapted to deal with other shapes in Chap. 5. The adaptations made to the original treemap algorithm enabled the subdivision of constraint convex shapes into smaller rectangular-based compartments, moulded by the referred constraint shapes. Some results are provided with the virtual reconstruction of real and fictitious ruins. In Chap. 6, the treemap approach is enhanced again to support the generation of buildings constrained by non-convex layouts, through the implementation of a technique that relies in a labelling approach used by Binary Space Partitioning (BSP) trees to define disposable parts, for further suppression. In this approach, BSP labelling approach was adapted to indicate holes in the floor plan, thus being renamed to fake-concave. Also in Chap. 6, a process for defining the shapes of inner rooms is proposed which consists in adding or removing constraint room walls to define a room shape.

After the space division step, the remaining floor plan is achieved in a process that is similar in every iteration of the subdivision approach: interior/exterior doors and windows are placed and 2D's expanded to occupy a certain wall portion. Finally, the 3D virtual model is produced through a set of extrusions, roof placement and detail completions, as it will be seen in this document.

The next sections will introduce the developed procedural modelling methodology, along with the supporting ontology.

3.2 Ontology for Buildings

This section addresses the buildings' ontology that is the first regulatory structure for the developed procedural modelling methodology, by establishing an organization concerning buildings and its integrating elements, from a generic viewpoint.

Accordingly to the ontology, a building is composed by temporary building part containers (for the arrangement of other building parts) or final building parts; each building part contains at least one floor; each floor is composed by divisions that can be temporary containers for room arrangements or final rooms. Transitions, such as doors and windows, can be related with floors or/and divisions. The buildings' ontology is partially based on the CityGML standard [7, 8] and provides the possibility of defining a sequential set of operations and also geometric transformations in agreement with each element, maintaining the coherence of the virtual model and generation control. The designed ontology was also extended to be used in the regulation of roman houses generation. A few more structures were added to support some particularities observed in the roman architecture such as columns, pools (*impluviums*) and roof openings (*compluviums*). Both of these ontological structures—generic and roman—will be explained next.

3.2.1 Generic Ontology

The buildings' generic ontology was defined considering an abstraction effort to identify and connect the architectonic elements that can be found in a building, regardless of era or style. Thus, it is defined that a *Building* structure is the root container that holds *BuildingPart* instances, that can be seen as horizontal compositions (parts of the same building distributed at the ground level). From this viewpoint, each tower belonging to a castle would be considered as a castle's building part, for example. In turn, each *BuildingPart* instance can have inner building parts for arrangement purposes or can aggregate one or more *Floor* structures which can be defined as the vertical parts of each building part. In other words, as a floor inherits from *BuildingPart*, floors can be seen as vertical building parts that rise inside a given building part. Each *Floor* structure contains a set of *Division* structures that can be rooms or temporary compartments for arrangement purposes. Divisions are typically connected to other divisions or to the exterior by transitions (equivalent to *Transition* structures), as for example doors and windows. Transitions share overlapping boundary surfaces (equivalent to *BoundarySurface* structures), belonging to different divisions or floors. These *BoundarySurface* structures represent the limits of a floor or a division, that can extend to *WallSurface*, *CeilingSurface* or *GroundSurface* structures. *AbstractElement* is useful to describe special architectonic features, such as columns, footers, portals or even furniture. Finally, the *Roof* represents the cover of each building part, usually placed in the top of the last floor. Figure 3.1 depicts the generic ontology schema.

To promote the reuse of features, specifically of the geometry and appearance, it was decided that each ontological element extends from the same father: *WorldObject*. Figure 3.2 illustrates the referred inheritance.

This ontology is a generic skeleton that integrates a set of empty definition classes to keep it structurally open to concrete adaptations to other supports, as for example, data models or ontology-based grammars.

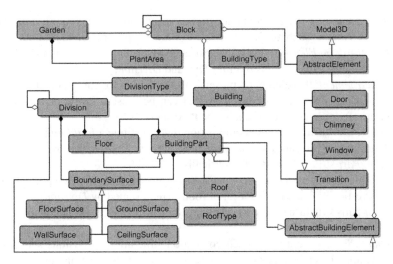

Fig. 3.1 Generic buildings' ontology: an abstract semantic schema that defines the connections between the elements that can be part of a building. A *Building* is composed by a set of *BuildingPart* structures; each *BuildingPart* is a stack of *Floor* structures; each *Floor* aggregates a set of *Division* structures; each *Transition* relates a *Floor* and a *Division* to define a transition to the exterior or two *Division* elements to establish a inner transition; A *Roof* is the cover of each *BuildingPart*; *BoundarySurface* defines a boundary for *Floor* or *Division* structures, as for example walls, grounds or ceilings. Other architectonic structures are considered such as gardens—represented by *Garden* class—or even 3D models foreseeing the use of complex furniture

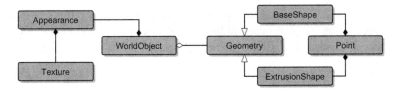

Fig. 3.2 The *WorldObject* parent and the inheritance mechanism. Each ontology element extends from *WorldObject*, that contains features common to each element, specifically, the *Geometry* and the *Appearance*

3.2.2   Generic Ontology Elements

The cityGML-based ontology contains a set of interrelated classes. This subsection will provide a brief description of each one of them:

- *WorldObject*: this is the base class for each ontological element. *WorldObject* contains a *Geometry* and an *Appearance*, which define an object shape and look, respectively;
- *Block*: represents the *Building* holding area. In other words, it can be seen as the exterior ground frame that will support *Building* structures;

- *Building*: this is a master container that describes edifications along with their internal elements, such as *Floor*, *Division* or *Roof* type structures;
- *AbstractBuildingElement*: this is the abstract base element that is contained by the *Building* class in the form of *BuildingPart* and *Division*;
- *AbstractElement*: this element represents an abstraction for complementary structures, such as ornaments or furniture that can be present inside or outside the *Building* (for example tables, chairs, beds, vases);
- *BuildingPart*: each horizontal composition that constitute a *Building* is identified as *BuildingPart*. It can also be specialized into *Floor*, which form a stack of *BuildingPart* structures that arise vertically;
- *Floor*: this class—used to represent a storey—inherits from *BuildingPart* to compose it vertically. It also holds a set of rooms (represented by *Division*);
- *Division*: this structure is used to represent compartments for arrangements or final rooms inside a *Floor*;
- *BoundarySurface*: represents each contention structure for divisions and floors. For example, it can be an exterior or interior wall and also a ceiling or a ground;
- *Transition*: represents a building hole that intends to provide an interface with the building exterior or a passage between a couple of divisions. A *Transition* can be a door or a window, for example;
- *Roof*: *BuildingPart* structures are covered by roofs, that are typically placed upon the highest floor;
- *Garden*: optionally, a *Division* may hold a *Garden*. These structures can also be present in the *Building* exterior, namely in its containing *Block*.

The abstractness of the generic ontology foresees the possibility of extending it to other particular cases (e.g. roman buildings), as it will be presented in the following subsection.

3.2.3 Extending the Generic Ontology to the Roman Architecture

The requirements of the roman architecture are more specific than those used to plan and develop the generic ontology. The existence of structures such as arches and columns calls for the specialization of some generic classes, mainly abstract elements. In this book, only a few roman elements were extended to demonstrate the flexibility and scalability of the buildings' generic ontology, through the inheritance mechanism. It is important to state that the roman architecture was not explored in-depth to maintain the focus of this book. Thus, the elements in Fig. 3.3 should only be considered for demonstration purposes.

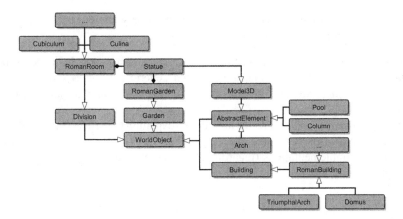

Fig. 3.3 The specialization of the generic ontology into roman architectural objects, by extending generic elements to fulfil some of the roman architecture requirements

3.2.4 Roman Ontology Elements

The specialized roman classes are described below.

- *RomanBuilding*: specifies an abstract building belonging to the roman style. A *domus* is an example of an ancient roman building, used for housing purposes;
- *Column*: this is very common in the roman style. *Column* structures were used for decorative or structural purposes, inside or outside the buildings;
- *Pool*: were used in *domus* for water recoil and supply. These pools, also called *impluviums* collected the water through the openings in the roofs and ceilings called *compluviums*;
- *Statue*: this structure represents tributes to ancient roman emperors. The complexity of this kind of structures makes them more suitable to be used as 3D models manually produced, in the context of virtual representations;
- *Arch*: similarly to columns, this element was very used as ornament in the roman architecture. This book does not cover the reconstruction of it. However, it should be considered as a likely extension example from *AbstractElement*;
- *RomanRoom*: this structure is an abstraction that intends to represent a division belonging to a roman building. *Culina* and *Cubicullum*, for example, are two division types that can be found inside a *domus*.

Summing up, the designed buildings' generic ontology intends to establish a generalist organization for edified structures, based on the CityGML standard. Moreover, it provides the first regulatory set for the procedural modelling methodology that will be presented in the next section. Additionally, it is possible to extend the generic ontology to define the organization of architectural elements for a specific architectonic style (for example, the roman style). Flexibility, scalability and re-usability are some of the advantages that accrue from the adoption of these semantic structures, if one considers the following aspects:

- In the same ontology (and architectonic context), extensions can be made to specialize structures (for example, the designed generic ontologies stablish that a *BoundarySurface* extends to *WallSurface*, *FloorSurface*, *GroundSurface* and *CeilingSurface*);
- Extension/derivation mechanisms also allow adaptation to particular architectonic styles, from previously created ones;
- Associated implementations (regarding, for example, geometry production) can be reused and enhanced.

3.3   Procedural Modelling Methodology Overview

The procedural modelling methodology addressed in this book defines the process to produce virtual representations of one-floored traversable buildings composed by arbitrary shapes. The aforementioned ontology that describes the building entity and its interior components to properly regulate that methodology, can be mapped by auxiliary structures such as a data model (e.g., XML) or a grammar. The resulting rules are then interpreted and transformed into 3D geometries using a procedural modelling process.

In short, the process begins with having the floor plan assembled, considering inner and outer transitions (doors and windows); afterwards, the walls are extruded, the roof is also generated and placed upon each horizontal building composition (*BuildingPart*); finally, some details are added to enhance the appearance of the virtual building model.

3.3.1   Building Floor Plan Definition

The initial focus of this procedural modelling process is the production of the floor plan generation that is defined through a treemap structure—encoded in rules—that, in turn, establishes the building parts and divisions belonging to a building. Following treemap's structure, the process starts by dividing the building constraint polygon into subareas that represent the space reserved for building parts (horizontal compositions). Then, for each building part, a floor is created. Each one of those floors is then subdivided into divisions (or rooms), taking into consideration a set of high-level requirements, that are defined on the existent input structure, i.e. the encoded treemap rules that establish the positions and dimensions used to adapt interior divisions constraint shapes. The next step in the process is reserved for the marking of transitions: exterior ports and windows that constitute the points of connection with the outside of the building and inner doors that ensure connectivity between divisions. Thus, considering the architectural project requirements, access doors and outer windows are properly marked in the marginal divisions that are in direct contact with the building's limits. Then, inner doors are also marked upon overlapping walls of communicating divisions. In the end of this stage, some alterations can be made to the resulting divisions, in order to adapt their geometry through the modification of their contour walls. In short, this modification consists in removing or adding points to a given boundary surface that represents the referred division contour wall, as will be explained later with more specificity.

3.3.2   Extrusion, Roofing and Completions

The walls' extrusion and the placement of ceilings, grounds and roofs provide the 3D virtual model, in its final form. The walls' extrusion regards the positions occupied by the doors and the windows. Then, accordingly to the geometric limits of each division, both the ground and the ceiling are placed. The roofs are also generated and placed to cover the building top, considering its building parts. Finally, some features are produced—such as frames for doors and windows, building base and roof skeleton coarsening—to enhance appearance of the 3D virtual building model.

3.4   Summary

An overview on the procedural modelling methodology that is about to be detailed in the following chapters was addressed. That methodology regulates the generation process through the defined buildings' generic ontology—partially based on CityGML standard—which is extensible to particular cases such as the roman style. The abstractness of the developed ontology allows its adaptation to specific data formats—such as data models or grammars—that provide input for the modelling process. Such input can be seen as a set of requirements, in which implicit hierarchical structure of treemaps establish arrangements for building parts and divisions (or rooms), respective weights of occupation and connectivity between divisions, guiding the aforementioned methodology in the production of the desired virtual building model. This is done through the application of the following sequence of steps: floor plan definition, wall extrusion, roof generation and placement and finally, building enhancements through the improvement of element details.

References

1. Béhé, F., Galland, S., Gaud, N., Nicolle, C., Koukam, A.: An ontology-based metamodel for multiagent-based simulations. Simul. Model. Pract. Theory **40**(0), 64–85 (2014). ISSN 1569-190X. doi:10.1016/j.simpat.2013.09.002. http://www.sciencedirect.com/science/article/pii/S1569190X13001342
2. Mignard, C., Nicolle, C.: Merging BIM and GIS using ontologies application to urban facility management in active3d. Comput. Indus. **65**(9), 1276–1290 (2014). ISSN 0166-3615. doi:10.1016/j.compind.2014.07.008. http://www.sciencedirect.com/science/article/pii/S0166361514001432. Special Issue on The Role of Ontologies in Future Web-based Industrial Enterprises
3. Dylla, K., Muller, P., Ulmer, A., Haegler, S., Fischer, B.: Rome reborn 2.0: a case study of virtual city reconstruction using procedural modeling techniques. In: Proceedings of Computer Applications and Quantitative Methods in Archaeology (2009)
4. Rodrigues, N., Dionísio, M., Gonçalves, A., Magalhães, L.M.G., Moura, J.P.: Rule-based generation of houses. Comput. Graph. Geom. **10**(2), 49–65 (2008). http://cgg-journal.com/2008-2/05/index.html
5. Rodrigues, N., Dionísio, M., Gonçalves, A., Magalhães, L.G., Moura, L.G., Chalmers, A.: Incorporating legal rules on procedural house generation. In: Proceedings of the 24th Spring Conference on Computer Graphics, SCCG '08, pp. 59–66, New York, NY, USA, 2008. ACM (2008). ISBN 978-1-60558-957-2. doi:10.1145/1921264.1921279
6. Maciel, M.: Vitrúvio - Tratado De Arquitetura. Ist Press (2006)
7. Gröger, G., Kolbe, T.H., Czerwinski, A., Nagel, C.: OGC City Geography Markup Language (CityGML) Encoding Standard. Technical report, Open Geospatial Consortium (2008)
8. Gröger, G., Kolbe, T.H., Nagel, C., Häfele, K.-H.: OGC City Geography Markup Language (CityGML) Encoding Standard. Technical report, Open Geospatial Consortium (2012)
9. Rau-Chaplin, A., MacKay-Lyons, B., Spierenburg, P.: The lahave house project: towards and automated architectural design service. In: Proceedings of the International Conference on Computer Aided Design (CADEX-96), pp. 62–66. IEEE (1996)
10. Martin, J.: Algorithmic beauty of buildings methods for procedural building generation. Computer Science Honors Theses, p. 4 (2005)
11. Lopes, R., Tim, T., Smelik, R.M., de Kraker, K.J., Bidarra, R.: A constrained growth method for procedural floor plan generation. In: GAMEON'10, November 2010. http://graphics.tudelft.nl/~rafa/myPapers/bidarra.GAMEON10.pdf
12. Rodrigues, N.: Rule-based generation of virtual traversable architectural-period houses. Ph.D. thesis, University of Trás-os-Montes e Alto Douro (2010)
13. Merrell, P., Schkufza, E., Koltun, V.: Computer-generated residential building layouts. ACM Trans. Graph. **29**(6), 181:1–181:12 (2010). ISSN 0730-0301. doi:10.1145/1882261.1866203
14. Tutenel, T., Smelik, R.M., Lopes, R., de Kraker, K.J., Bidarra, R.: Generating consistent buildings: a semantic approach for integrating procedural techniques. IEEE Trans. Comput. Intell. AI Games **3**(3), 274–288 (2011). ISSN 1943-068X. doi:10.1109/TCIAIG.2011.2162842
15. Marson, F., Musse, S.R.: Automatic real-time generation of floor plans based on squarified treemaps algorithm. Int. J. Comput. Games Technol. **2010**, 7:1–7:10 (2010). ISSN 1687-7047. doi:10.1155/2010/624817
16. Mirahmadi, M., Shami, A.: A novel algorithm for real-time procedural generation of building floor plans. CoRR abs/1211.5842 (2012)
17. Bruls, M., Huizing, K., van Wijk, J.: Squarified treemaps. In: Proceedings of the Joint Eurographics and IEEE TCVG Symposium on Visualization, pp. 33–42. Press (1999)
18. Hahn, E., Bose, P., Whitehead, A.: Lazy generation of building interiors in realtime. In: Canadian Conference on Electrical and Computer Engineering, 2006, CCECE '06, pp. 2441–2444, May 2006. doi:10.1109/CCECE.2006.277767
19. Hohmann, B., Havemann, S., Krispel, U., Fellner, D.: A GML shape grammar for semantically enriched 3d building models. Comput. Graph. **34**(4), 322–334 (2010). ISSN

0097-8493. doi:10.1016/j.cag.2010.05.007. http://www.sciencedirect.com/science/article/pii/S0097849310000749. Procedural Methods in Computer Graphics Illustrative Visualization

20. Leblanc, L., Houle, J., Poulin, P.: Component-based modeling of complete buildings. In: Proceedings of Graphics Interface 2011, GI '11, pp. 87–94, School of Computer Science, University of Waterloo, Waterloo, Ontario, Canada, 2011. Canadian Human-Computer Communications Society. ISBN 978-1-4503-0693-5. http://dl.acm.org/citation.cfm?id=1992917.1992932

21. Dahl, A., Rinde, L.: Procedural Generation of Indoor Environments. Master Thesis with shared authorship, Charmers University of Technology (2008)

22. Johnson, B., Shneiderman, B.: Treemaps: a space-filling approach to the visualization of hierarchical information structures. In: Proceedings of the IEEE Conference on Visualization, 1991, Visualization'91, pp. 284–291. IEEE (1991)

Chapter 4
Generation of Virtual Buildings Formed by Rectangles

Abstract This chapter presents the first stage of the procedural modelling methodology addressed in this book, which is capable of generating *domus*—ancient roman houses—considering rectangular constraint shapes, through the combination of an ontological schema—extended to support some elements of the roman architecture—and a treemap-based procedural modelling process, that is responsible for creating the geometry according to the rules that define the buildings.

The first version of the procedural modelling methodology addressed in this book focus the generation of roman houses with rectangular-based floor plans. It must first receive the proper guidelines containing the building definition rules. Besides their relation with the ontology, a part of these guidelines follow a proper L-System format to enable the creation of a hierarchical treemap, establishing the division and subdivision of the building into building parts and divisions (also known as rooms). More specifically, the L-System approach is used to iterate through the rules to mount the treemap that hierarchically organizes the subdivision of the building into a node system, mapping building parts and their divisions. Afterwards, the splitting of the building floor plan into areas occurs, considering the previous treemap definition: the rectangle that constraints the building is assumed as a root node, that is divided into building parts, where each building part is subdivided into divisions. Division sizes are calculated considering the occupation weights explicitly provided by definition rules that will be addressed further in this chapter. The floor plan generation process is over when transitions are created to properly connect divisions and to define buildings' access doors and windows. Restriction rules are used for this purpose, since they specify connections between division types. Next, the walls are extruded and finally roofs are created. Some typical roman structures were included, such as columns and pools (*impluviums/compluviums*) to render the virtual houses properly adapted to the roman architecture context.

© The Author(s) 2016
T. Adão et al., *Ontology-based Procedural Modelling of Traversable Buildings Composed by Arbitrary Shapes*, SpringerBriefs in Computer Science, DOI 10.1007/978-3-319-42372-2_4

4.1   Preliminary Procedural Modelling Methodology

In this section, the earlier stage of the procedural modelling methodology for *domus* generation is presented, considering the roman ontology addressed in Chap. 3, definition rules and restriction rules.

The roman ontology results from the extension of some elements belonging to the designed generic ontology presented in Chap. 3. Based on it, an L-System rule format to define treemaps for building subdivision was developed. The referred rule format belongs to the definition rules which also define division occupation weights, division types, building and building part dimensions and roofs. The subdivision process occurs hierarchically: first, building parts are divided and then, for each divided building part, inner divisions are also subdivided. There is another type of rules set—restriction rules—that imposes a complementary level of guidelines: it establishes the types of division that can connect.

Regarding the procedural modelling methodology, it starts with the floor plan production. First, the subdivision of the building into building parts and division areas, oriented by the aforementioned definition and restriction rules, takes place. Then, considering the second set of rules, adjacent divisions are properly interconnected, ending the floor plan generation step. A sequence of extrusions results in the 3D virtual model of a *domus*.

4.1.1   Ontology Integration

The generation of roman structures requires adaptations to the previously addressed generic ontology. However, its core—semantics and organization—remains unchanged. The main container element continues to be the *Building*. Typically, buildings are composed by, at least, one *BuildingPart*, each one holding a single *Floor* and a unique *Roof*. In turn, each *Floor* groups a set of divisions, connected to each other through transitions, that also represent building interfaces, such as exterior access doors and windows.

The required ontology adaptations to support roman structures involve the extension of some of its elements. Thus, to support the particular case of the roman *domus*, the following main extensions were made: *Domus* inherits features from *RomanBuilding* which is, in turn, a *Building* extension; *RomanRoom* inherits features from *Division*, that is a base class for several other specific structures such as *Cubiculum*, *Culina*, *Vestibulum*, *Atrium*, etc.; to support the generation of divisions similar to *atriums* with the typical structures for water recoil purposes, the *AbstractElement* gave origin to *Pool* which, in turn, represents the *Impluvium*, a water deposit that looks like a tank; *Compluvium* is a special *Transition*, usually aligned with an *Impluvium* structure, that represents a hole in the roof for water capturing; finally, *RomanGarden* inherits features from *Garden*, to support the generation of a backyard inside *Perystilium* divisions. Figure 3.3 (Chap. 3) depicts the aforementioned inheritances.

4.1.2   Methodology Regulation: Definition Rules

Some rules have to be defined to specify a mandatory set of parameters regarding the floor plan generation, specifically the treemap that subdivides the building into building parts and divisions, dimensions related with the building layout and building parts, divisions' categorization by functional zones, occupation weights regarding the different building elements and presence of structures inside the divisions.

The first referred definition rules set represent the guidelines to divide the building area—one of the main steps regarding floor plan generation—combining two main concepts: treemaps and L-System. The L-System that specifies the set of building parts, arrangement containers and final divisions is, in fact, an encoded treemap structure which is iteratively and recursively mounted.

The first axiom corresponds to the treemap root node regarding the constraint rectangle of the building. The subsequent symbols can be one of two types: replaceable or final. The former corresponds to building parts (i.e. distinguishable vertical building structures that group division sets) or division containers (i.e. section for arrangement purposes). The later symbol type maps final divisions. The process is considered complete when there are no more symbols to replace. Rules defining the treemap are specified by means of grammar with the following format:

```
SemSymID: ResultSemSym0, ResultSemSym1, ...,
          ResultSemSymN
```

SemSym represents the axiomatic symbol that gives place to the resulting symbols that come after a colon punctuation mark (:). In general, symbols enable the distinction of ontological elements, depending on functional zone categorization (addressed later in this subsection). Thus, building part containers are represented by symbols without an attributed functional zone category that point to other uncategorised symbols (expressing other building part containers or final building parts). Final building parts are represented by terminal symbols without a functional zone relation, that point to division symbols having a functional zone category. In turn, division containers and final divisions are expressed by symbols with a functional zone category that are replaceable and terminal, respectively.

Building dimensions are also specified in the definition rules. The size of the footprint and the maximum building height are defined as the following:

```
BuildingDimension: value_footprint_x,
                   value_footprint_y,
                   value_of_max_height
```

Another kind of definition rules aims the categorization of divisions sets (specified in the treemap definition rules) as private rooms, central spaces, inside and access corridors and also stores. Such categorization intends to generalize the division types

Table 4.1 Roman *domus* divisions categorized by functional zones

Category / Division	Access corridor	Central space	Private room	Inside corridor	Store
Atrium		✓			
Cubiculum			✓		
Triclinium			✓		
Tablinium				✓	
Andron				✓	
Peristylium		✓			
Vestibulum	✓				
Cullina			✓		
Bathroom			✓		
Oecus			✓		
Exedra			✓		
Alae			✓		
Servae			✓		
Tabernae					✓

in functional zones, while establishing an implicit relation with the ontology. The general format for division's categorization is the following:

```
Category: Division0, Division0, ..., DivisionN
```

In the specific case of roman *domus*, divisions can be categorized as following: *Vestibulum* is identified as a corridor; divisions such as *Cubiculum*, *Triclinium*, *Cullina* and *Bathroom* are considered private rooms; typically, a *domus* has two central spaces identified as *Atrium* and *Peristylium*; *Tablinium* and *Andron* are inner corridors; finally there are stores used for business known as *Tabernae*. Table 4.1 depicts this categorization.

Thereby, those division types have to be used when defining a certain roman division, rather than the original designation. For example, a certain symbol specified in the treemap rules with the goal of being an *atrium* should be declared in this category rules as a central space.

Along with the treemap defining building parts, building dimension and division categories, weights of occupation must be specified, using the following format:

```
Weights: ElementA-0.5, ElementB-0.5
```

The keyword *Weights* marks the beginning of this specification set. In this set, identifier names must be concordant with the elements specified in the treemap specification. Ensuring that, an occupation value for each element can be established using a hyphen mark (-) to separate element from value. The occupation value refers to the relative area that is occupied by a certain element inside its parent (it corresponds to the launcher axiom specified in the definition rules). For example, two building parts can occupy a relative value of 0.5 from a building footprint and each building part can be fulfilled by four different divisions, each one taking a relative value of 0.25 from the available area.

There are also the extrusion rules. Keyword *BpartsHeight* starts a rules section where the heights of each building part can be defined, in the following format:

```
BpartsHeight: BuildingPart0-valueA,
              BuildingPart1-valueB, ...,
              BuildingPartN-valueX
```

In this scope, building parts are symbols pre-specified on definition rules that have the respective height value, separated by hyphen (-). The height value is a relation between each building part and the total height of the building, previously defined. Let us say that, if hypothetically a building is defined with 4 of height and a building part has a relative height of 0.8, this building part has an absolute height of 3.2. Thereby, different heights for the different constituent building parts based on relative values can be defined.

Some divisions might be attached with inner structures such as pools or gardens. To define those divisions and the respective structures, the following rules set needs to be properly specified:

```
StructureA: DivisionA, DivisionB, ..., DivisionX
StructureB: DivisionC, DivisionD, ..., DivisionZ
```

The aforementioned rules specify the list of divisions that hold a certain structure (*ImpluviumCompluvium* and *Garden* are the supported ones). The structure designation comes before a colon punctuation mark (:) which is followed by a list of divisions (symbols previously defined in the treemap rules).

Finally, roofing rules define which kind of roof covers each building part. The keyword *Roof* marks the beginning of roof definitions that are specified in the following format:

```
Roof: BuildingPart0-RoofTypeA,
      BuildingPart1-RoofTypeB, ...,
      BuildingPartN-RoofTypeX
```

After a colon (:) mark, a set of symbols coupled by hyphens (-) defines, for each building part, the covering type of roof.

4.1.3 *Methodology Regulation: Restriction Rules*

This rules define a complementary set of guidelines and default restrictions used for methodology regulation. Essentially, they specify the set of possible connections between different functional zones categorizing divisions (Fig. 4.1) and textures for coating each ontological element.

The restriction set that aims to specify the pair of division types that can connect are encoded as the following template format:

```
Connections:  Category0-Category1,
              Category0-Category2, ...,
              CategoryX-CategoryY
```

Connections are specified after the keyword *Connections* which is followed by a set of division pairs, separated by comma (,). Each division in a given pair is connected to the other by an hyphen mark (-).

Finally, texturing rules define the coating of each ontology element. They are specified using the keyword *Texture* and then, after a colon (-) mark, the pairs of elements and textures as the following template rule:

```
Texture:  OntologyElement0-texture1.jpg, ...,
          OntologyElementN-textureX.jpg
```

4.1.4 *Procedural Modelling Approach*

The procedural modelling approach uses as input the aforementioned rules and performs a set of steps that aim to achieve a building's virtual representation. The main stages regard the production of the floor plan (subdivision and then, connection between resulting division) and the extrusion of walls. They will be addressed in the following topics.

Fig. 4.1 Representative schema of the connections possibilities between functional zones, that regulate the methodology for generating building based on rectangular floor plans

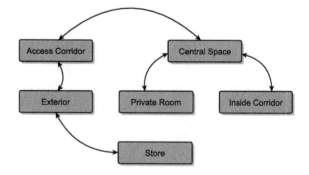

Fig. 4.2 Result of a treemap approach used for dividing a roman *domus* into rectangular divisions. This floor plan follows the suggestions made by Rodrigues [1] regarding the layout of a typical roman house, i.e. a *domus* with an *atrium* and a *peristylium*

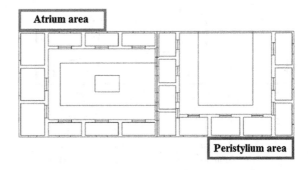

(A) Floor plan subdivision:

The first two steps of the floor plan subdivision are related with the treemap— implicitly encoded in an L-System subset provided by definition rules—that aims the subdivision of the building layout into rectangular areas, resulting in building parts and divisions (Fig. 4.2). Specifically and considering the subdivision treemap, the first iteration splits the building's initial area into smaller squares which are the building parts. The areas of the building parts are then divided into smaller areas for divisions (which include corridors). The splitting process performs divisions, in each case, accordingly with the relative weights (in percentage), specified in the definition rules.

(B) Division connections:

When the splitting process is complete, a graph to connect adjacent divisions based on functional zones classification and considering restriction rules is created. This graph is used in the fourth step to mark the openings between connected divisions, that must be adjacent. Afterwards, division wall segments interfacing with the building's exterior layout are marked with entry doors for the divisions identified as being access corridors or stores. Moreover, the divisions that have available wall segments placed upon the exterior building layout are properly marked with windows. The next step alters the geometry of each division and each building part to properly adapt to the marked doors and windows: the line that sets the limits of a division is segmented around the transitions. Wall thickness is also applied in this step, along with the marking of roof openings, if needed. These openings are applied to enable the communication between structures such as *impluvium* and *compluvium*, that constitute a water recoil system in the context of the roman architecture. The result of these steps is a rule-concordant floor plan.

(C) Extrusion process:

The procedural methodology finishes its execution by extruding the resulting floor plan, to produce a 3D virtual building model. This process achieves its objective in a few steps. First, divisions' walls and building parts are raised from segments that do not overlap to openings. Then, wall portions belonging

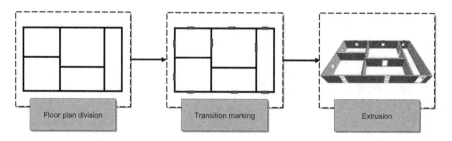

Fig. 4.3 Procedural modelling approach main stages, from the treemap-based floor plan division to the walls' extrusion. From *left* to *right*, the first frame depicts the subdivision of a given rectangular footprint, based on treemap. Then, the second frame exposes the flagging of doors and windows. The last frame shows the walls' extrusion stage, that considers the previously flagged transitions

to openings are properly extruded: if dealing with a door, a set of walls rises to glue the top of the transition to the building's roof base; the same happens for a window, but additional walls are raised to patch the window bottom. The process respects the restrictions imposed by the previously addressed definition rules. Some other elements are extruded to complete the virtual building. For example, columns are raised from the ground to the ceiling of their holding divisions. Finally, the roof is produced through a set of extrusions properly applied accordingly with its type: Hip, Mansard, Flat, or Holed.

Figure 4.3 presents a scheme that depicts the aforementioned process.

After the presentation of this methodology's main stages, an algorithmic perspective will be provided, to detail each one of those stages.

The first one regards the treemap subdivision. After the proper loading of the tree into a set of ontology-based objects with the data provided by definition rules, the building footprint is determined and *BuildingPart* structures gain their definitions along with their respective *Division* structures. Then, this tree is traversed to perform the subdivision. The terms *horizontal* and *vertical* (and lexically related) are used to identify a certain orientation in a 2D plane, during this floor plan division explanation. The process starts by horizontally splitting the building footprint into rectangles for *BuildingPart* structures (direct child nodes of the root node representing the *Building*). Then, a splitting orientation flag is changed to vertical on each one of those *BuildingPart* structures to alter the splitting direction of their subsequent *BuildingPart* children, if they exist. The presence of *BuildingPart* child instances inside a given *BuildingPart* instance converts the parent into a temporary container for arrangement purposes. Temporary *BuildingParts* can have many depth levels with more temporary *BuildingPart* structures that vary the splitting orientation (inverted relatively to its holding structure) in each depth. If a given *BuildingPart* instance does not possess any *BuildingPart* child, it is considered a final piece (last depth building part) with an established position and dimension.

The same operating logic applies to the *Division* structures, defined inside each final *BuildingPart* instance. They start by splitting, horizontally, each *Division* instance area. The orientation flag is also changed to enable the divisions' arrangement during the subdivision: a feature achieved with disposable temporary *Division* structures (as it occurs with the *BuildingPart* structures). The presence of inner child instances of *Division* converts a given *Division* parent into a temporary container (subsequent structures are also converted, recursively, if they hold children of the same type). Otherwise, the absence of them indicates that a given division is a final structure.

In short, a building can have one or several temporary *BuildingPart* containers which, in turn, arrange other temporary containers of the same type or final *BuildingPart* structures. Each *BuildingPart* structure may hold several temporary *Division* containers and the latter can have other structures of the same type or even final *Division* instances. *Division* or *BuildingPart* children represent deeper levels of structures that invert the splitting orientation on those children, from depth to depth.

For both cases, *BuildingPart* and *Division*, temporary structures used in splitting operation are removed at the end of the subdivision process because they are no longer needed. Figure 4.4, depicts the generic workflow that addresses the aforementioned operations.

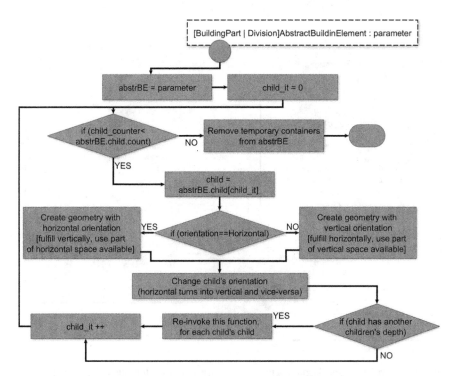

Fig. 4.4 Generic workflow diagram depicting the behaviour of the treemap subdivision process. When a given *AbstractBuildingElement* structure has child instances of its same type, a rectangular area for each one of those children is produced, considering the respective occupation weights and subdivision orientations (vertical or horizontal). Then, each child is submitted to the same operations to recursively process the children of that child, if they exist. In the end, all parent structures (temporary containers with children of the same type) are disposed while the final structures (without children) are kept. The process works for both *BuildingPart* and *Division* structures

The creation of transitions is the next stage to complete the floor plan definition. First, the division type is checked for each *Division* inside each *BuildingPart*. If the *Division* is identified as an access corridor or store—division types that require access to the building from the outside—then an entry door is properly created upon the first available division wall segment overlapping with the building constraint polygon. Moreover, the remaining segments that overlap with the building constraint polygon are used to mark windows. Finally, adjacent interior divisions that connect with each other (requirement defined on the restriction rules for connectable division types) are marked with a common interior door. Figure 4.5 presents the behaviour of the transition placement stage.

During the floor plan generation, other structures might be marked to adapt and enhance the virtual building model. These operations rely in some definition rules

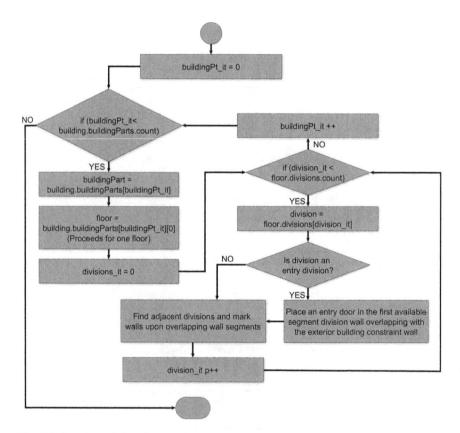

Fig. 4.5 Generic workflow diagram depicting the behaviour of the transition placement process. The *Division* structures are traversed inside each *BuildingPart* to proceed with the placement of entry doors, windows and interior doors. This step relies, mainly, in the identification of overlapping wall segments between two *Division* structures or between a given *Division* and the building constraints, to properly create transitions

regarding the attribution of structures to divisions (addressed previously). A division attributed with an *ImpluviumCompluvium* flag is endowed with both *Impluvium* (pool for water collection) and *Compluvium* (roof opening for water recoil) structures which are geometrically marked in the centre of the referred division rectangular area, along with a set of surrounding columns. Typically, a *domus* division with such structures is an *atrium*, in the context of the roman architecture. Moreover, a division required to have a *Garden* is provided with that homologous structure and the respective geometric definition. Thus, a garden area is geometrically marked in the centre of the division rectangle along with a set of surrounding columns. Such *domus* division is known as *peristyliums*, in the context of the roman architecture.

After determining the transitions and their positions and dimensions, a set of extrusions takes place. This step enhances the virtual building with a 3D aspect. Essentially, the walls of the constituting *BuildingPart* and *Division* structures are raised around the previously marked transitions. Some wall patches are then applied

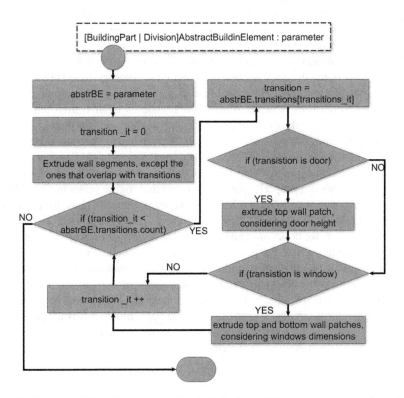

Fig. 4.6 Generic workflow diagram depicting the behaviour of the extrusion process, for a single *AbstractBuildingElement*. Each *AbstractBuildingElement* (*Division* or *BuildingPart*) is subjected to an extrusion process that consists in raising its respective walls, considering the previously marked transitions, which have to be patched to achieve the representation of the "wall hole" adapted to both cases windows or doors

to doors (top) and windows (top and bottom) segments to properly complete the surrounding interior and exterior walls. Figure 4.6 depicts the extrusion process.

Afterwards, some elements are extruded to complete the virtual model. This is the case of the existing *Column* set and *Garden* structures. Finally, each *BuildingPart* instance is covered with a proper roof type, ending the virtual building production.

4.2 Implementation Prototype

An application to implement this preliminary methodology version was developed. In the first interaction, rules must be provided and properly encoded in a simple text file. The text file that contains the encoded rules is composed by two sections: definition rules and restriction rules. The first rules set contains the treemap-based structure for the arrangement of building parts and divisions, occupation weights, building dimensions, building parts heights, roof definitions and attribution of special structures to divisions while the latter restrictive rules set establishes the functional zones that can connect and describe the coating textures for building elements.

The application starts by interpreting the definition rules—with a format based on L-systems—to mount the treemap, that is structured in ontology-based class objects. In other words, the building holds a set of building part containers and final building parts that, in turn, group a subset of division containers or final divisions. Those containers are temporarily used for grouping and arrangement purposes, as it was already underlined in previous sections. Then, the subdivision process takes place: containers, building parts and divisions are split considering the tree mapped into the object classes and also the respective occupation weights. After area provisioning, doors and windows are properly marked in a step that highly relies in the connection rules—a subset of restriction rules—and adjacent division. Thus, for each final division, it is checked—through rules consultation—if its neighbours are suitable for a connection: if so, doors are marked between the proper division pairs that are stored in a "visitation list" for future checkings and redundancy avoidance. Entry doors and windows might also be marked in the division wall segments that overlap with the building constraints (i.e. exterior walls' segments), following the process described in previous sections. Next, the walls are extruded respecting the transition marks. Frames for doors and windows are created and finally, roofs are produced. Some additional structures are included—such as columns and pools—to enhance the *domus* with roman architectural elements.

4.3 Preliminary Tests and Results

A *domus* was defined—using the aforementioned rule sets—to demonstrate the methodology capabilities in this earlier stage of development. A text file containing definition rules was manually encoded to establish building parts, the divisions belonging to each one, their occupation weights and arrangements, division categorization, and roof definitions. The following excerpt exposes an L-system based specification, defining a treemap for the subdivision of building parts and their respective divisions:

```
Line1  -> Domus:Bpart0,Bpart1
Line2  -> Bpart0:SectionBpart0V0,SectionBpart0V1
Line3  -> SectionBpart0V0:Tabernae,Vestibulum,
          Cubiculum
Line4  -> SectionBpart0V1: SectionBpart0V1H0,
          SectionBpart0V1H1,SectionBpart0V1H2
Line5  -> SectionBpart0V1H0:Cubiculum,Cubiculum,Alae
Line6  -> SectionBpart0V1H1:Atrium
Line7  -> SectionBpart0V1H2:Cubiculum,Cubiculum,
          Noroom
Line8  -> Bpart1:SectionBpart1V0,SectionBpart1V1,
          SectionBpart1V2
Line9  -> SectionBpart1V0:Triclinium,Tablinium,Andron,
          Cubiculum
Line10 -> SectionBpart1V1:SectionBpart1V1H0,
          SectionBpart1V1H1
Line11 -> SectionBpart1V1H0:Peristylium
Line12 -> SectionBpart1V1H1:Vestibulum,Cullina,
          Bathroom
Line13 -> SectionBpart1V2:Oecus,Exedra,Oecus
```

Line1 establishes that a *domus* will be composed by two building parts (x-axis aligned), *Bpart0* and *Bpart1*. *Line2* states the definition for two new auxiliary containers inside *Bpart0* (the alignment resets to x-axis every time a new structure type is being divided through definition rules, except for auxiliary containers): *SectionBpart0V0* and *SectionBpart0V1*. The former will be populated with three y-axis aligned divisions, as it is defined in *Line3*. The latter is set to be redivided into new three y-axis aligned auxiliary containers, accordingly with *Line4*. *Line5*, *Line6* and *Line7* establish the rules for the referred containers, that are intended to become final x-axis aligned divisions. *Line8* rules define the division of *Bpart1* into three auxiliary containers (x-axis aligned): *SectionBpart1V0*, *SectionBpart1V1* and *SectionBpart1V2*. The first one will give place to four y-axis aligned roman rooms, accordingly with *Line9* rules. The second is set to have a new redivision in *Line10*, also aligned with y-axis, which will result in two auxiliary containers. *Line11* and *Line12* define the set of x-axis aligned divisions that will replace both the last referred containers. Lastly, *SectionBpart1V2* is overwritten with three final divisions or rooms (y-axis aligned), due to *Line13* rule.

Other definition rules, such as divisions occupation weights, flags for entry divisions, windows, division connections and roof types, were also specified. After reading the encoded rules, the prototype performs a set of steps—detailed in previous

Fig. 4.7 Final layout of a generated *domus* including interiors and a exterior, using the prototype created to test and validate the preliminary methodology version for generating virtual building models based on rectangular floor plans. The virtual model contains a set of *domus* divisions, including some typical ones representing the *atrium* and the *peristylium*

sections—to achieve the 3D virtual model. A rectangular footprint is subdivided into a floor plan using a treemap approach that respects the L-system structure for division arrangement. Then, doors and windows are properly marked on the divisions. Finally, a set of extrusions along with the roof placement, results in the virtual building which is shown on Fig. 4.7.

4.4 Summary

In this chapter, an ontology-based solution for procedural generation of ancient structures, specifically roman houses—*domus*-configured by rectangular floor plans, was presented. The solution implements a working methodology that relies on an abstract ontological specification for buildings, foreseeing the possibility of extension to other architectonic styles. The entire generation process relies in a set of rules—definition and restriction rules—to successfully achieve the proper virtual building 3D model.

However, this procedural modelling methodology needs to overcome the key issue related with the treemap approach: the generation of buildings exclusively configured by rectangular shapes. The next chapters will focus on this issues, seeking to contribute with a solution to overcome them. A XML-based rule system will also be suggested as an alternative for providing virtual buildings' production rules.

Reference

1. Rodrigues, N.: Rule-based generation of virtual traversable architectural-period houses. Ph.D. thesis, University of Trás-os-Montes e Alto Douro (2010)

Chapter 5
Generation of Virtual Buildings Constrained by Convex Shapes

Abstract The second procedural modelling methodology version that will be addressed in this chapter has a modified treemap-based approach that enables the generation of virtual buildings with floor plans constrained by convex polygons. Other improvements include the input rules simplification and the incorporation of a moderation process to validate each input set (regarding syntax and geometry).

In this chapter, the second version of the procedural modelling methodology is presented. It requires a set of input definition rules—complaint with the requirements of an ontology-based data model—to trigger the building's generation process. The preliminary validation of the input rules is made through a moderation process responsible by checking for errors (format and typos) and pre-testing the defined transitions at a geometric level. The resulting ontology-based class set, properly loaded with validated rules, passes through the procedural modelling process that, in turn, builds the expected virtual model in the following sequence of steps: constraint polygon determination; division area provisioning considering division classification, which is an extended feature for division type differentiation (e.g., kitchen or living room); placement of windows and exterior access doors; placement of transitions between divisions; roof generation; placement of ceilings and floors and finally, virtual model detailing.

For concept-proof purposes, a software system was developed. It accepts XML files properly loaded with building's data as input—designated by eXtended Markup Language for Building Definition (XML4BD)—and implements the aforementioned processes in two main modules: (1) the rules moderator module and (2) the procedural modelling module.

5.1 Enhanced Procedural Modelling Methodology

The previously addressed procedural modelling methodology version (Chap. 4) was only capable of generating virtual buildings based on rectangular floor plans and also composed by rectangular divisions. In this section, some improvements to

© The Author(s) 2016   63
T. Adão et al., *Ontology-based Procedural Modelling of Traversable Buildings Composed by Arbitrary Shapes*, SpringerBriefs in Computer Science,
DOI 10.1007/978-3-319-42372-2_5

that methodology are going to be presented, namely those concerning the definition rules and the treemap-based subdivision process of the building's constraint polygon. These improvements enable the generation of virtual buildings constrained by arbitrary convex shapes.

5.1.1 Ontology-Based Data Model to Guide Definition Rules

The definition rules presented on the past Chap. 4 are effective in specifying virtual buildings. However, the used format is complex because involves a lot of required definitions with a considerable amount of parameters specified using some heterogeneous formats: first, an L-system based specification has to be defined with the treemap of temporary containers (symbols that express arrangement purpose structures), building parts (terminal symbols without a functional zone category) and divisions (terminal symbols with a functional zone category); those specified divisions must be categorized by functional zone as well as division containers; each one of those elements has to be properly configured with occupation weights; buildings and their constituting parts require the specification of dimensions (heights, widths and lengths); roofs were also required for definition. The whole information set has to be defined using several subsets of non-intuitive grammar-based rules which have a structure that is not clearly engaged with the designed ontology. Besides, there are no mechanisms for validating them. Thus, in an attempt of simplifying virtual buildings definitions and make them prone to proper validation, an ontology-based data model was established with a straight structure and a clear field set regarding buildings data. Two main achievements are reached with this strategical change: the specification based on L-system structures was replaced by the ontology-based specification which relies in the establishment of explicit node hierarchies between the several elements composing a virtual building (temporary containers, building parts and divisions); finally, occupation weights are automatically populated based on a size factor defined only for final divisions (explained in detail in later sections) in order to replace the tedious task of defining occupation weights for each building element individually.

The aforementioned simplified ontology-based data model was designed considering a set of fields that were identified as having the essential information about a building. As it might be noticed in Fig. 5.1, its entity classes and organization respect the ontology defined for buildings from which it derives. A *Building* represents the major container of the scope, since every other objects are, directly or indirectly, supported by it. A *Building* instance holds at least one or more *BuildingPart* instances. In turn, each *BuildingPart* instance may hold one or more *Floor* instances (however, it is assumed that buildings with only one floor will be addressed). A *Division* instance is essentially the most elementary compartment of a building: an interior room with a purpose (e.g. sleep or cook). In turn, one or more *Division* instances are grouped by *Floor* instances. Moreover, a division can aggregate structures: *Pool* and *Garden* are the ones currently supported.

For arrangement purposes both *Division* and *BuildingPart* can hold spawned instances of the same entity class: a *Division* container can be temporarily used for arranging other *Division* instances (temporary or final) inside it as well as *BuildingPart* containers are able to do with other inner building parts. Finally, *Transition* represents windows and doors. They compose *BuildingPart* and *Division* instances to let them keep track of their transitions. Each *Transition* also keeps track of the structure pairs sharing it (more relevant for interior divisions).

The presented data model intends to constitute a guiding structure for the specification of definition rules. Hereafter, the fields contained in each entity class will be exposed and briefly explained.

(A) Building:
   Building is the main container structure and it is composed by the following fields:

   - ID: represents the unambiguous identifier field;
   - name: refers to the building name;
   - description: refers to the building description. It can be used as a complementary information field;
   - type: identifies the building type (e.g. habitation house or commercial building).

(B) BuildingPart:
   A building part represents the horizontally displaced parts of the building (dis-

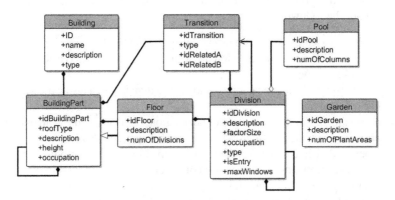

Fig. 5.1 Simplified ontology-based data model. In concordance with the building ontology, it is established that a *Building* holds a *BuildingPart*. In theory, a *BuildingPart* supports one or more *Floor* instances. However, the procedural modelling methodology addressed in this book only covers the generation of buildings composed by a unique floor. *Floor*, in turn, is composed by a set of *Division* instances. *Transition* instances are shared and tracked by *BuildingPart* and *Division* instances. *Pool* and *Garden* structures can make part of a division. There is also the possibility of creating *BuildingPart* and *Division* containers to arrange other *BuildingPart* and *Division* instances inside those containers, respectively

tributed at the ground level). It can also be seen as a sub-container, holding floors. This entity class is composed by the following fields:

- idBuildingPart: represents the unambiguous identifier field;
- roofType: defines the type of the covering roof. The supported types are *Flat, Pyramide, Hip, Mansard, MansardHoled* and *None*;
- description: refers to the building part description. It can be used as a complementary information field;
- height: specifies building part height (useful for extrusions);
- occupation: refers to the weight of occupation, relatively to the available floor plan area (value determined with the set of divisions).

(C) Floor:
A floor is a container for divisions (or rooms). The fields specified in this entity are:

- idFloor: represents the unambiguous identifier field;
- description: refers to the floor description. It can be used as a complementary information field;
- numOfDivisions: it is a numeric field that can be set with the number of supported divisions.

(D) Division:
Division is one of the most elementary structures inside a building, consisting of the interior portion of the floor. Usually, they connect to other structures of the same kind foreseeing the mobility inside the virtual building. Its structure includes the following fields:

- idDivision: represents the unambiguous identifier field;
- description: refers to the division description. It can be used as a complementary information field;
- factorSize: refers to the factor used to grow a division area inside the available floor plan area;
- occupation: refers to the weight of occupation, relatively to the available floor plan area (obtained from growth operations using factorSize);
- type: the divisions might be generic rooms, bedrooms, living rooms, corridors, kitchens, toilets or even temporary containers;
- isEntry: this is a flag that indicates if a division instance is an entry division or not (accessible from the exterior).
- maxWindows: refers to the maximum windows number that a given division can have. However, the effective number of windows can be lesser, depending on the number and length of the available wall segments overlapping the building's constraint shape (explained with a bit more detail in later sections).

(E) Transition:
Transition instances define the interior doors connecting two adjacent divisions, entry doors or windows:

- idTransition: represents the unambiguous identifier field;
- type: window, door or entry door are the supported types that particularize a transition;
- idRelatedA: specifies the first entity instance (e.g. *Division*) involved in the transition sharing;
- idRelatedB: specifies the second entity instance involved in the transition sharing;

5.1.2 Definition Rules

To define a building, a set of definition rules must be provided in conformity with the designed ontology-based data model. These rules aim to specify a set of nodes with a hierarchical organization. Each node can represent a building part a division or even a temporary container for arrangement purposes (for divisions or for building parts). All of them have a set of required fields that constitute parameters used in the procedural generation stage. For example, a node representing a final division must define an id, size factor, occupation value (it can be set with 0 since it will be supplanted with a value resulting from the operations regarding the growth and balancing of rooms based on size factor, explained with higher detail in later sections) division type (room, bathroom, kitchen, etc.) and also an entry door flag (true or false whether an access door to the building exterior is required or not in a given division). A further section reserved for methodology implementation will present a concrete XML format for buildings definition, structured in concordance with the addressed data model.

5.1.3 Restriction Rules

Restriction rules were defined, in Chap. 4, as belonging to a complementary grammar that is used to specify textures for building elements and allowed connections between division types. These rules, which became independent from definition, are now represented by default parameters used by the procedural modelling methodology in strategic steps of building's generation. The list bellow specifies some of the more important ones, briefly:

- Texture parameters (based on the generic ontology): are used to define the coating texture of each ontology element.
- scale thickness: value used for the scale of the interior outlines relative to the exterior layout (which results in the gap between these walls that represents the wall thickness);
- small room default: relative size factor for small rooms, considering the building layout area;

- small room min: min. of occupation factor that a small room may achieve;
- small room max: max. of occupation factor that a small room may achieve;
- medium room default: relative size factor for medium rooms, considering the building layout area;
- medium room min: min. of occupation factor that a medium room may achieve;
- medium room max: max. of occupation factor that a medium room may achieve;
- big room default: relative size factor for big rooms, considering the building layout area;
- big room min: min. of occupation factor that a big room may achieve;
- big room max: max. of occupation factor that a big room may achieve.

At this point, connections are no longer established by restriction rules (or default parameters). Instead, they are specified in definition rules for the sake of building definition freedom.

5.1.4   Moderation Process for Definition Rules

Definition rules moderation constitutes the first regulation instrument before a virtual building model generation. It is responsible for reading input rules and for validating their structure against the ontology-based data model. Afterward, a class set that maps the ontology accordingly with the data extracted from the input rules is loaded. This step has a pretest that relies on floor plan probing to check its feasibility. More specifically, this step intends to ensure that every connectable divisions supports a transitions door. Otherwise, transitions are dropped for connectable divisions that do not share an adjacent wall with sufficient length to have it.

Floor plan probing is achieved in three main steps: first, all virtual building elements (including divisions, building parts and temporary structures) occupy a floor plan area that is based on their size factors; then, the first floor plan subdivision takes place; lastly, a step responsible for balancing divisions' occupations takes place to validate the placement of transitions between connectable divisions. These steps are presented in detail hereinafter:

(A) Setting the occupations of virtual buildings elements based on size factors: first, floor plan's occupation areas are properly set among divisions considering their size factors, i.e. occupation areas are increased and adjusted using jumps of size factor until the sum of all occupations equals 1. Moreover, division sizes affect their wrapping structures (building part containers, final building parts and division containers), recursively: the occupation value of each wrapping structure is obtained adding up their inner structures' occupation values (provided by final divisions to all the other wrappers), as shows Eq. 5.1.

$$container.occupation = \sum_{i=0}^{n} container\_child[i].occupation \qquad (5.1)$$

(B) Floor plan subdivision: this step must be highlighted as it is extremely relevant to the enhanced procedural modelling methodology. It is used to create areas for divisions and building parts accordingly with their previously calculated occupations. Since convex shapes are not controllable as rectangles, some adjustments are required to achieve the approximated occupation area inside the restriction polygon. Such adjustments involve shape intersections, division area measurements and small increments and decrements to the division areas. This will be explained in detail in the next subsection.

(C) Balancing division weights (to try) to ensure transitions: entry and connecting divisions are tested to check if their weights and the arrangements are properly set up. This checking operation consists of verifying if all of the connecting divisions own a common shared wall with enough space to place a door. Moreover, division weights can be increased and/or decreased dynamically using a "borrow space" approach to try to satisfy the referred condition. Problematic transitions, which failed the checking operation are suppressed to avoid further geometrical issues in the procedural modelling process. A failed check occurs when two connecting divisions reach their expansion limit (minimum and maximum limits are provided by a subset of restriction rules) and still there is no space for a transition. Figure 5.2 depicts the process in a generic workflow. Lastly, divisions' occupation values in the floor plan are recalibrated with the new definitions for temporary containers and building parts.

5.1.5 Procedural Modelling Generation Process

After the moderation process validating input definition rules to ensure the proper loading of the ontology-based class set and after probing and adjusting the building's floor plan definitions, the procedural modelling process takes place and starts by producing the floor plan for a given restriction polygon. Each building element—which can be a container for arrangement purposes, a building part or a division—is placed and adjusted to the building constraint convex polygon. Essentially, the process follows a treemap subdivision with some intersection and dimensioning operations to deal with the division of such convex polygon.

The footprint division process is iterative and begins with a rectangle for each iteration and building element. The area of this element's initial shape is calculated with the occupation weight value, previously obtained in the rules moderation process. However, an intersection has to be made in order to adapt the element's rectangular shape to the virtual building layout, which can result in a partial loss of element's area. This occurs when the rectangular shape overlaps the border of the building's constraint polygon. Afterwards, Heron's formula is used to calculate the area of the new element's shape resulting from the intersection (through internal triangles): if the current occupation weight is lesser than the weight required by the rules, then the process is repeated from the first step, with a wider rectangle (dimensioned with

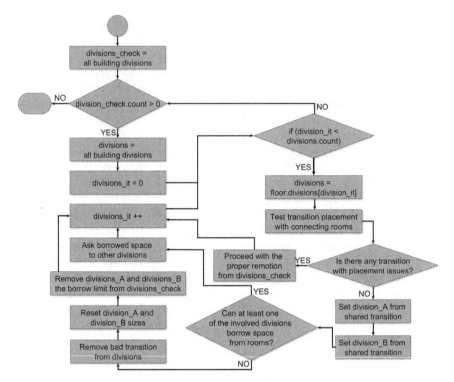

Fig. 5.2 Workflow depicting the process of balancing division weights through space borrowing. Initially, a checklist with the complete final virtual building divisions is loaded for control purposes. Then, each division in the building is subjected to the transition placement test which involves a given division (in the iteration) and also their neighbours. If the test does not return any problematic transition (lack of space in placing), the tested division is removed from the checklist along with the neighbour divisions with exclusive connection to the tested division. Otherwise and if at least one of the involved divisions support expansion, a small portion of space (based on size factor) is asked to other divisions. To lend space, requested divisions must ensure that they support area decrease (based on the limits established by the restriction rules), without impacting their own transitions. On the other hand, if the tested and connected divisions already reach their limit for expansion, they are both removed from the checklist, sizes are rolled back and returned to their origin divisions and the problematic transition is suppressed. The process is repeated until the division checklist is empty

an increment of 0.1 % of the virtual building layout area). Otherwise, the process is considered finished for the current virtual building element and the next one is processed with the same set of operations.

To achieve the complete floor plan, doors and windows are marked considering the division graph provided by the input definition rules, similarly to which was described in the previous chapter. Thus, interior doors are placed on the overlapping wall segments belonging to pairs of connectable divisions, while access entries and windows are placed in the margins of the building constraint polygon, regarding the flagged divisions for this purpose.

The extrusion of the elements provides a 3D model definition. The process is highly based on the previously determined floor plan. Thus, inner and outer walls are raised until a certain height, provided by input definition rules. Then, frames for doors and windows are created along with the roof. Some details such as roof skeleton coarsening, building base and division footers are also created to enhance the virtual model realism.

This summarizes the procedural modelling generation process. Each referred step will now be presented in greater detail:

(A) Restriction Polygon:
   The polygon that constraints the virtual building is provided by input rules and used to wrap interior divisions. This polygon consists in a list of points that follow a (x, y, z) format. The detection of a non-convex polygon triggers a convex hull operation to force this requirement.

(B) Combining treemap and greedy approach to perform floor plan subdivision:
   The floor plan is achieved in two stages: first, a convex area is split to produce the divisions' layout and then those divisions are connected. The ontology-based class structure (previously loaded) follows a treemap organization that provides informations on how to split the area by specifying a hierarchical organization for the subdivision operation and the respective occupation weights. Treemap-based floor plan subdivision is properly adapted to deal with the irregularity of the constraint polygon in this enhanced methodology version.
   In this stage, the virtual building constraint polygon is recursively split to adapt building parts and divisions, following a recursive treemap approach. Next, a more detailed explanation about the splitting process is presented.
   Let a given building part A in the treemap-based class structure be waiting to be partitioned in its child divisions. Let the orientation of the process be vertical and let A be described by a convex geometry coincident with the building constraint polygon. For each child division in A, a rectangular area is created considering its occupation weight (relatively to the virtual building area which, in this example, is the same as A area). This rectangular area is set to fill the available horizontal area and to use a part of the vertical area to partially or totally fit A space, depending on the child division weight value. Then, the rectangle is affected with the intersection result of the current division shape with the containing element (A, in this example) shape, in an operation that is prone to losing division area, specially in the building layout margins. Such possibility calls for an area compensation process. The established one relies in iterative dimensioning operations until the desired division area is reached. Thereby, the post-interception shape area is measured using Heron's formula (5.2), which relies in the internal triangles' areas calculation:

$$A\Delta = (\sigma(\sigma - \alpha) * (\sigma - \beta) * (\sigma - \chi)), \tag{5.2}$$

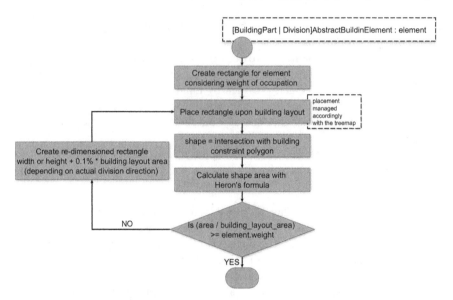

Fig. 5.3 General workflow depicting the adjustments made to a given building element during the floor plan division process of a virtual building constrained by a convex shape (valid for building parts, divisions and temporary containers). In the first place, a rectangular area is created considering the element's occupation weight. Then, the rectangle is intersected with the building's constraint polygon, resulting in a new polygon. The intersected polygon area is calculated to determine if it has the desired size: if so, the process ends; otherwise, the process is reapplied using a wider rectangle (that grows in each iteration) until the desired building element area is reached

where α, β, χ represent the lateral sizes of each triangle and σ the semi-perimeter given by Eq. 5.3:

$$\sigma = (\alpha + \beta + \chi)/2 \tag{5.3}$$

If the resulting area occupies less than the specified current division weight, a wider rectangle is created for the division and tested from the placement and intersection stages. This is a cyclic process that lasts until the division area reaches the proper weight inside the container layout and consequently within the building constraint polygon (Fig. 5.3). Afterward, the process is also applied for every other divisions in this vertical container, changing their splitting orientation to horizontal, as it was previously explained in Chap. 4, during the description of the treemap approach. If they hold some inner divisions to split, the process occurs with other splitting direction. Nodes belonging to these child nodes follow the same splitting process with vertical orientation and so on, recursively and iteratively, until the end of the treemap-based class structure.

The process to produce the floor plan layout is exemplified in the Fig. 5.4. It depicts a treemap definition and the respective area splitting process occurring upon the virtual building constraint polygon. Figure 5.4a depicts a treemap

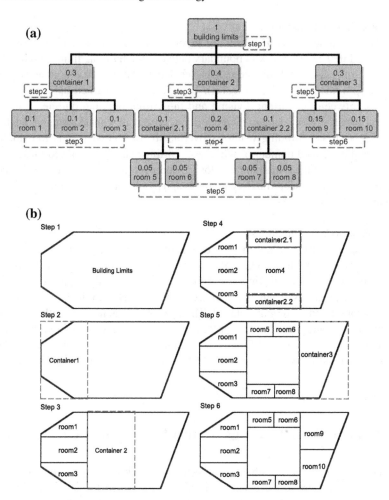

Fig. 5.4 Example of a treemap structure defining a floor plan arrangement and respective floor plan subdivision process. **a** Presents an example of a treemap structure defining a floor plan arrangement (explicitly provided by definition rules). **b** Depicts the respective floor plan subdivision process based on the presented treemap definition. This schema depicts a set of steps representing the splitting process based on treemap. The first step is to find the total container which matches the outer limits. The second step places the *container 1* and iteratively finds and adjusts the polygon that results from the intersection with the virtual building outer bounds until the required occupation weight is reached. In the third step, the same process occurs inside *container 2*, but this time to place and expand final rooms (alias for divisions). In the remaining steps, the same process is applied until the final floor plan is obtained (sixth step)

schema based on data loaded from definition rules. Figure 5.4b depicts the process of floor plan subdivision guided by the previously presented treemap definition.

(C) Placement of transitions:
   After dividing the virtual building layout, the entry doors and windows are
   marked in the common wall boundary between the building limits and the division limits. For each division, it is verified if the entrance door is required
   (flag provided by definition rules). If so, a door is marked upon the shared
   wall between the current division and the virtual building outline. Then, the
   windows are also placed in the common shared wall, considering the available
   space and also avoiding windows overlap. If the shared wall is too small to
   place the planned number of windows, a fitting subset is achieved through the
   suppression of the remaining windows. Moreover, inner divisions are also connected by doors, accordingly with the graph provided by definition rules, in the
   earlier stages.

(D) Virtual model completions:
   The walls' extrusion and the placement of the ceiling, ground and roof provides the 3D final form. The walls' extrusion operation considers the positions
   occupied by doors and windows. Thus, the extrusion only happens around the
   defined transitions. Then, accordingly to the geometric limits of each division,
   the ground and ceiling are placed. The roof is also generated with the proper
   dimensions and placed at the top of the virtual building (individually for each
   building part) to cover it. Finally, some features—such as doors and windows
   frames or building base—are added to the 3D virtual model to increase its
   realism.

5.2 Enhanced Methodology System Implementation

A system implementing the enhanced procedural modelling methodology and capable of generating virtual traversable buildings constrained by arbitrary shapes is
presented in this section. Input definition rules are provided through XML4BD files
that have a structure highly based on the designed building data model, previously
addressed in Sect. 5.1.1. Within this system, there is a rule moderator module that
implements the moderation process addressed in previous sections. This module
checks both the XML4BD syntax and organization, loads the informations into a
class structure that maps the ontology-based data model and filters inconsistencies,
at the floor plan level, related to transitions placement. After proper validation, the
previously loaded class structure is forwarded to the procedural modelling module which generates the virtual building, considering a set of default parameters—
independent from the definition rules—that specifies architectonic constraints (e.g.
wall thickness). The architecture of the presented system is shown in Fig. 5.5.

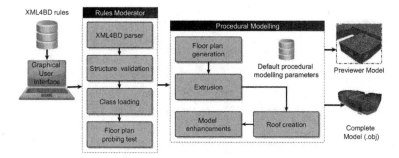

Fig. 5.5 Architecture of the system that implements the methodology for generating buildings constrained by arbitrary shapes, considering XML4BD specifications as input rules. The system contains a Rule Moderator module to validate XML input files and also a procedural modelling module to generate the geometry of the virtual building

5.2.1 An Ontology-Based XML for Virtual Buildings Definition (XML4BD)

The structure of the adopted XML format, designated XML4BD, follows the ontology-based data model structure depicted by Fig. 5.6. Thus, inside the building node, it is defined the constraint polygon and building parts (horizontal compositions of the building) are defined. Inside each building part node a set of floors can be specified (although the procedural modelling process only deals with buildings containing building parts with a single floor) and inside each floor node there is a group of divisions. Inside the virtual building node are also defined the connections between divisions. Each node that is part of the referred XML4BD structure is strictly related to the previously addressed data model (Sect. 5.1.1) regarding both semantics and data structure.

5.2.2 Rules Moderator Module

A rules moderator module incorporates this system to validate the XML4BD files (input definition rules) regarding its syntax and organization. This module is also responsible for loading an ontology-based class structure—implemented considering the aforementioned data model presented on Sect. 5.1.1—with the proper data. After that, floor plan probing takes place to check the transitions of connecting divisions: the ones that do not fit are dismissed.

The process regarding rules moderation, presented in the previous Sect. 5.1.4, is closely related to the steps performed by this module, as it intents to point the following items:

(A) Rules validation: initially, the input XML file is parsed to check inconsistencies on structure and writing. On the one hand, misplaced nodes are used as indi-

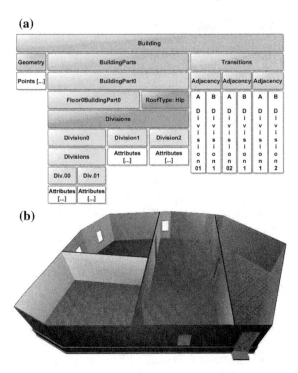

Fig. 5.6 Example of a XML4BD node system and resulting 3D virtual model. In **a** an example of a XML4BD node system is depicted. The building root node has a nested *buildingpart*, a set of points representing the constraint polygon and a list of transitions (nested set of nodes specifying inner divisions' connections). That building part node contains a nested floor node— *Floor0BuildingPart0*—with four divisions: besides final division *Division1* and *Division2*, there is also a *Division0* which is a temporary container for two other final divisions: *Div.00* and *Div.01*. In **b** the resulting virtual building, composed of one building part and four connecting divisions is shown

cators of malformed structures. On the other hand, writing inconsistencies are filtered through the detection of unrecognised symbols or wrong specification types (for example, it is expected a numeric value for parameters that define the maximum number of windows per division). These errors are then properly returned to the user, stopping system's execution until new demands;

(B) Class loading: this step is reached when the input file is in full agreement with the ontology-based data model and there is no inconsistencies to overcome. Its execution aims the creation of the building instance as well as its composing elements in a class structure that faithfully maps the previously presented data model;

(C) Floor plan probing test: the instances of the resulting ontology-based class structure are subjected, by the rules moderator module, to some operations that have the goal of correcting instance parameters, specifically the ones regarding the floor plan generation. Thus, the execution of this task starts by testing if the connecting rooms belonging to a given building have sufficient space in their common wall segments to hold a transition. The pairs of connecting rooms that do not fulfil this requirement are provided with space from other rooms (available to borrow), in an attempt of making a larger adjacency for placing a transition. The ones that reach the borrow limit are reset to their starting sizes and their failing transitions are deleted to avoid further issues in the procedural generation module.

After performing these steps, this module releases the class set to the procedural modelling module, addressed in the next subsection.

5.2.3 Procedural Modelling Module

The aim of this module is to semi-automatically generate virtual building models. Its operation is very similar to an automatic housebuilder when constructing a given building by following the architectural plan orientations whereas in this case, information is provided through XML4BD definition files. Thus, the procedural modelling module uses the class structure previously loaded and duly verified by the rule moderator module to obtain virtual building's definitions. Among those classes, there is a set of mandatory data that includes the polygon that defines the virtual building limits, their constituting divisions and respective organization, their occupation weights in the restriction polygon and also the connections between them. Considering those definitions, this module starts a progressive process to produce a 3D virtual building model.

The first step regards the floor plan generation process and groups four operations: constraint polygon determination (must be convex, otherwise the module forces this requirement using a convex hull algorithm), floor plan area division (according to the loaded class structure based on XML4BD rules), placement of external doors and windows and lastly the placement of connecting doors between divisions (correspondent to the graph defined in class structure, loaded from XML4BD input file). The walls' extrusion step will raise the walls in the virtual building, considering its transitions. The few last steps will generate grounds, ceilings and roof, thus completing the 3D virtual building model.

Some tests involving ancient structures were made to demonstrate the effectiveness of the developed system while applying the procedural modelling methodology to generate virtual buildings constrained by convex shapes. The next sections focus these tests along with the achieved results.

5.3 Preliminary Tests and Results

The first trials consisted of generating missing ancient buildings based on textual descriptions [1]. After analysing the available texts provided in Conimbriga's website [2], a set of ontology-based XML files (a pre-release of XML4BD) were set up with the most relevant information found in those online documents (e.g. restriction polygon and division arrangements). Then, these files were submitted to the procedural modelling system to generate the complete geometry of the buildings, including its exteriors and interiors. Results are presented in Fig. 5.7.

A few pilot experiments were made (besides the previously addressed test to reconstruct missing buildings) to demonstrate the capabilities of the procedural modelling methodology system in generating traversable buildings constrained by arbitrary shapes. A set of XML4BD files were populated with data to simulate fictitious ancient structures. These buildings were projected to be outlined by arbitrary convex polygons. Each building has different configurations, with distinct building parts, divisions, size factors, arrangements, connections and structures. The involved complexity ranges between a simple building with four inner divisions and a more complex edifice having several divisions and an inner garden. Each XML4BD file is provided as input to the system and validated by the rules moderator module, which results in an ontology-based class structure properly loaded with building's data.

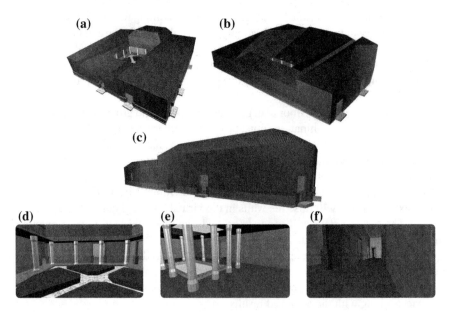

Fig. 5.7 Reconstructed roman buildings of Conimbriga (Portugal): the exterior and interior of the house of skeletons are presented in (**a**) and (**d**), respectively; **b** and **e** depict the exterior and interior of the house of fountains; finally, **c** exposes the exterior facades of the via south stores, while **f** shows part of its interior

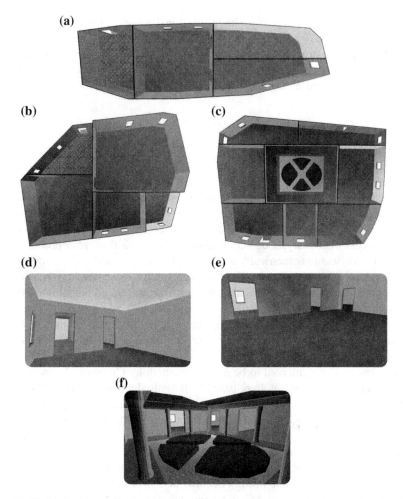

Fig. 5.8 Fictitious virtual building models representing ancient roman structures and produced by the system that implements the methodology for generating buildings constrained by convex shapes. Three different XML4BD files were defined to trigger the generation of the following buildings: two simple houses—**a** and **b** with four and five divisions, respectively, and a third house—**c** with eight divisions, including one that contains a central garden

These classes are then processed by procedural modelling module, which produces the 3D virtual building. The verified XML files tested followed the format addressed on Sect. 5.2.1.

Specifically, three buildings were defined accordingly with the XML4BD format. All of them are constrained by different convex polygons with variable dimensions. The first building is the simplest one. It includes a kitchen—the access division (or room) of the building—which is connected to a hall that conducts to a bedroom and also a bathroom. Then, a second building is presented with an entry kitchen connected to a living room which also contains a passage to a wider generic room. Generic room interfaces with a bedroom and also a bathroom. Finally, the last building includes five rooms (final divisions), a kitchen and a bathroom. At the center, there's a division that holds a special structure: a garden with four plant areas and also columns. The garden division connects all other division. Figure 5.8 shows the graphical results of the XML4BD files processing.

5.4   Summary

This chapter presented the enhanced version of the procedural modelling methodology addressed in this book which, at this point, is capable of producing 3D traversable buildings constrained by convex polygons. A rule moderation process was also established to filter syntax and structuring errors in rules. Moreover, this moderation process also analysis divisions' connectivity with floor plan probing tests that enable to discard geometrically unsupported transitions and avoid errors in further procedural generation stages. The module result is a clean ontology-based class which is then converted into a virtual building by the procedural modelling process. The floor plan generation is the first stage and employs some operations to deal with convex constraint shapes delimiting the building. Lastly, the complete virtual 3D building model is achieved through a set of extrusion and enhancements (e.g. transitions' frames).

A system was implemented to be used as methodology's proof of concept. The system receives as input an ontology-based XML—also known as XML4BD—which contains the definitions of a given building, including its related building parts, floors, divisions and transitions. The file passes through a XML4BD (rules) moderator module that reads and validates the XML4BD structure. The referred moderator also loads an ontology-based class structure and performs a few tests to ensure the coherency related with the floor plan (e.g. elimination of transitions between divisions that do not share a common wall). Then, the action of the procedural modelling module takes place. This module iterates through the class structure to produce 3D virtual models from the floor plan step until the last model enhancements.

The performed tests to the system demonstrated the versatility of this tool in creating buildings with several configurations and topologies. Results pointed out that this tool is effective in producing buildings constrained by pure convex shapes. Besides, it is also possible to include in the building special divisions holding inner structures, like pools or gardens with columns.

This methodology has still, however, some limitations: the generation of floor plans does not support holes (absence of geometry) and the division's shapes cannot be altered. The next chapter presents the final procedural modelling methodology, by addressing these issues. Moreover, a stochastic approach for the random generation of buildings is addressed as an experimental attempt of automating the methodology.

References

1. Adão, T., Batista, R., Peres, E., Magalhães, L.G., António, C.: Reconstructing traversable build-ings for archaeology with eras. In: Proceedings of the Virtual and Networked Organizations: Emergent Technologies and Tools—ViNOrg '13 (2013)
2. Correia, V.: Conimbriga ruínas - museu monográfico. http://www.conimbriga.pt/portugues/ruinas0.html, 2002. Accessed January 2014

Chapter 6
Generation of Virtual Buildings Composed by Arbitrary Shapes

Abstract This chapter presents the final version of the procedural modelling methodology which works with an ontology-based grammar. Its procedural modelling process supports the generation of virtual buildings delimited by non-convex shapes, with divisions constrained by a variable number of delimiting wall segments. Furthermore, an experimental graph-based stochastic process that bridges with this methodology to enable the production of virtual random buildings is covered.

The final version of the procedural modelling methodology works with an ontology-based grammar and supports the generation of virtual buildings delimited by non-convex shapes, with divisions constrained by a variable number of delimiting wall segments. To have a fully automatic generation of virtual building models (with minimal user inputs) a stochastic process is presented. Specifically, two types of stochastic requests can be made with a proper input set: for an expeditious generation of a random buildings' set, the desired number of buildings has to be provided; alternatively, to generate a building with a specific divisions set and configuration, a list enumerating those divisions has to be submitted along with the desired building configuration (L-shaped, U-shaped or fully convex). For each generation task, the aforementioned stochastic process arranges the rooms (or divisions) by priorities, mounts the graph of connecting divisions and randomly arranges them in a node structure that mimics a tree map. Therefore, this node structure is then transformed into grammar rules that are used to properly produce a 3D virtual building model, using the final procedural modelling process.

A procedural generation system was also developed to implement the procedural modelling methodology in its final version. Within this system, two tools—deterministic and stochastic—were developed. The former relies on user floor plans drawings alongside with its parametrization. The latter permits the expeditious generation of random virtual buildings through computer-managed selection, based on two possible types of user inputs: a restrictive list of divisions and building configuration or the desired number of buildings to be generated. As a result, both tools produce a set of ontology-based grammar rules (or consecutive sets, in the case of user request for random buildings production through the stochastic tool). Then, those rules pass through the couple of system's modules to be properly processed.

T. Adão et al., *Ontology-based Procedural Modelling of Traversable Buildings Composed by Arbitrary Shapes*, SpringerBriefs in Computer Science, DOI 10.1007/978-3-319-42372-2_6

After grammar rules validation and floor plan probing (pre-adjustment trial to ensure the connectivity between divisions and/or discard useless transitions), a sequence of steps is performed to achieve the 3D virtual model. The first step regards the floor plan generation, where the building's constraint polygon is recursively divided to create division areas. After defining all of the division areas, the number of wall segments is adjusted accordingly with the grammar rules requirements, which is also an enhancement in this final methodology version. The next step is to place transitions between divisions. Afterwards, the extrusion is applied to both interior and exterior walls and, finally, the roof, division ceilings and grounds placement occurs. Resulting buildings may be outlined by non-convex shapes through the application of a "fake-concave" technique in the aforementioned floor plan subdivision step.

6.1 Final Procedural Modelling Methodology

In Chaps. 3 and 4, the treemap approach was suggested to generate virtual buildings composed by rectangular shapes and constrained by convex limits, respectively. Some enhancements made to these versions led to the final procedural modelling methodology version in which a process for producing virtual traversable 3D building models composed by a single floor and constrained by arbitrary shapes is presented. The ontology addressed on Chap. 3 is still used for regulation purposes.

Based on the aforementioned ontology, a grammar is also specified in this chapter, establishing the latest form of definition rules for buildings. Each set of these rules consists in a per building specification in which the treemap of building parts and divisions is defined, as well as transitions and other relevant features like divisions' occupation weight and building parts' heights. Moreover, a new rule type that enables the specification of disposable building parts integrates this ontology-based definition rules. Such rule type is applied in the floor plan generation stage to delete building parts marked as disposable, as it will be explained later. Then, a verification stage—similar to the one presented on Chap. 5—debugs the grammar-based definition rules, regarding structure and typos. After validation, these rules are used to properly load an ontology-based class structure which is then subjected to a probing stage to ensure the feasibility of the floor plan. The probing stage consists in balancing division's occupation weights to make room for transitions or dispose the ones that cannot be placed between connecting divisions (already addressed on Chap. 5). At this point, the class set is ready to be submitted to the procedural modelling process that aims to produce the final 3D building model.

The aforementioned process occurs just like it was explained in the previous chapters. The initial goal of this process is the floor plan generation and the first step for this accomplishment consists in dividing the building's convex polygon into building parts—effective or disposable—and divisions, through a recursive treemap approach and considering the input definition rules. For each building part a floor is created and then subdivided into divisions. At the end of the building's polygon division step, the building parts marked as disposable are removed from the floor plan on which the following transformations may occur

- if all of the removed building parts overlap the floor plan's constraint polygon (the same as building's constraint polygon), such polygon becomes non-convex;
- otherwise, holes are created somewhere in the middle of the floor plan, i.e. the floor plan is set to have "dead" areas without any geometrical definition;
- the excluded middle event results in a floor plan with holes and constrained by a non-convex polygon.

This technique was named as "fake-concave" and uses a labelling approach based on BSP trees to define disposable elements. A new step is introduced in this procedural modelling process before the transitions markings: wall segments are adjusted to inner divisions, considering the definition rules provided through the grammar and associated parameters. The next step is to mark doors, windows and to connect divisions. Afterwards, external access doors and windows are marked in the proper divisions, more precisely in the division walls' segments that are in contact with the building limits. Then, the doors are also marked between overlapping wall segments of connecting divisions. Subsequently, walls are extruded considering the previously marked transitions. Those transitions also assume a 3D look with frames properly adapted to fit doors or windows. Ceilings and grounds are also created and next roofs for each building part are generated accordingly with the type indicated on the grammar. Finally, the virtual model is completed with some enhancements such as division footers, roof skeleton coarsening and stair steps for entry doors.

6.1.1 Ontology-Based Grammar

The previously settled definition rules (Chap. 5) resulted from a data model containing a set of essential fields that aimed to characterize a building. In this section, a grammar was designed to define virtual buildings, considering the works of many other authors who decided to use grammars in procedural modelling [1–7]. This grammar is highly based on the designed building's ontology, even regarding the structure, making it different from the one presented on Chap. 4.

The semantic scheme defined by the ontology constitutes the first regulatory structure for the presented procedural modelling methodology, creating the awareness of a generic building composition: buildings parts per building, floors per building parts, divisions per floor and related transitions such as doors and windows. This structure provides the possibility of defining a regulated sequence of operations and also the geometric transformations according to each element, while maintaining the coherence of the virtual model (see Chap. 3 for more details). The referred ontology was extended with some fields—regarding building's information—aiming the elaboration of an ontology-based grammar.

The ontology-based grammar definition recovers two concepts used on Chap. 4 L-system [8] and treemap [9]. The L-System is used to iteratively produce transformations through the symbols which are context free. However, transformations made to the symbols are "constructor functions" designed to operate considering ontology conventions. These transformations are also known as production rules and follow a logic sequence to achieve the building definition which comprises the number of vertical building parts and related floors, the divisions contained by each floor and also the connections between these divisions. Considering those structures a treemap of ontology-based objects is progressively mounted.

Everything starts with the building axiom, which is decomposed in building parts and transitions. Each building part is decomposed in floors and floors are then subdivided in divisions. Divisions and transitions are final symbols, with no decomposition. The referred production rules follow the format

```
axiom->function(_parameters):{resulting_symbols},
```

where axiom is the symbol under processing, the function is the ontology-based operation and the *resulting_symbols* constitutes the set of resulting symbols that should be processed in later steps. The ontology-based grammar functions are presented next.

(A) *Building*: this function, defines a building's constraint polygon. The resulting derivations include building parts and transitions.

- building(size(x,y,z)): assigns a rectangular area for the building;
- building(list(point(x,y,z), point(x,y,z), ...)): defines a building with a constraint polygon. The constraint polygon is a parameter expecting a set of points;
- building(generate_hull(num_points, width_min, width_max, aspect_ratio_ min, aspect_ratio_max)): defines a building constrained by a random polygon, generated with a number of cloud points, minimum and maximum width and also a minimum and maximum aspect ratio (used to determine the buildings length).

(B) *BuildingPart*: the *BuildingPart* function defines containers for space arrangement purposes or horizontal building compositions. The use of this function produces two types of derivations: on one hand containers produce another set of axioms defining *subbuildingparts* while, on the other hand, final horizontal compositions originate the floor axiom.

- buildingpart(roof_keyword, height_float): is used to define a buildingpart where roof_keyword defines the roof type that will cover the building part (possibilities: Flat | Pyramide | PyramideHip | Hip | Mansard | Combination | Gable | PorchHoled | None | MansardHoled), the height_float establishes the height of the building part. A building part with a height of 0, is a hole on the building (useful to create, for example, L or U-shaped building formats). The resulting symbols are related with floor definitions;
- buildingpart(): is used to define a container for other building parts, changing the axis of generation. If the building part is associated to a horizontal subdivision (x-axis), then its children should be divided following a vertical

composition (z-axis) and vice versa. This function returns a set of symbols related with sub-building parts.

(C) *Floor*: function regarding the floor definition requires the specification of the height for both the floor base and a secondary exterior wall. This function derives symbols for inner divisions.

- floor(base_height, exterior_wall_height): defines a floor with an exterior base and a secondary exterior wall. It retrieves a set of division symbols.

(D) *Division*: similarly to building parts, it is also possible to create division containers and final divisions (rooms) using *Division* functions.

- division(num_wall_segments, size, division_type, special_structure, is_entry, num_windows, footer_height, topunion_height): this function declares a division with a fixed number of wall segments (if *num_wall_segments* is lesser than 4, the number of wall segments will remain unchanged which means that the container shape and also the adjacent divisions will define the number of wall segments of this division; otherwise, division's wall segments will be added or deleted in order to fulfil the requirements of the input parameter), a certain size (small | medium | big), a division type (room | corridor | kitchen | toilet | hole), special structure (garden [supported by the generic ontology] | pool [supported by both the generic and the roman ontology] | none), a boolean specifying if a division should have a transition to the exterior and a height value for the bottom footer and for the header ceiling junction. It does not produce any axioms;
- division(): with this function, it is possible to create subdivisions inside a division, just like it is done with building parts. The function should retrieve a set of axioms for its child divisions.

(E) *Transitions*: this function defines the graph of inner divisions, i.e. provides a way of specifying the connectivity between divisions in order to ensure the circulation inside the virtual building.

- transitions(list(transition(d1,d2), ...)): it specifies the connections between the divisions belonging to the virtual building. This function works upon a final axiom defining the list of divisions that should be connected in the building.

6.1.2 Moderating Ontology-Based Grammar Rules

The moderation process presented in Chap. 5 was adapted to fit this ontology-based grammar format. First, each grammar-based instruction set is verified to check typos (unknown syntax) and structure (sequence conformity). Then, a floor plan probing is performed to ensure that the weights and the divisions arrangements are properly set up, using the same operations addressed in the moderation process presented in Chap. 5. Thus, connecting divisions are preliminarily tested with the placement of transitions upon overlapping divisions' wall segments. Those that do not fit trigger weight borrowing process among divisions. When space collection reaches the limit—provided by the restriction rules specified on Chap. 5—in a given couple of connected divisions, one of two events might happen: if the transition fits it is considered valid; otherwise, the transition is discarded to avoid malformed geometries in further operations, specifically those regarding procedural modelling.

6.1.3 Procedural Modelling Generation Process

The procedural modelling process starts by considering the properly validated virtual building definitions, provided by a set of grammar-based definition rules in order to obtain its working requirements. The mandatory data provided by this set includes the polygon that defines the building's limits, the virtual building constituting divisions and respective spatial organization, the weights of occupation of each division in the restriction polygon and the connections between them.

Once the floor plan definition is determined, a progressive process is triggered to produce the virtual building model. The initial steps are common to the ones described in previous procedural modelling methodologies versions: first, the restriction polygon is determined and forced to be convex; in the next step, the floor plan subdivision takes place to divide the virtual building polygon into smaller areas, according to grammar specifications.

At the rules definition time, building parts can be marked as empty—height equals to 0—which means that they will be disposed after the floor plan division. This results in a geometric hole that changes the contour shape that constraints the virtual building. This "fake-concave" technique, depicted in Fig. 6.1, relies on the BSP trees labelling approach to define disposable building parts.

A new step is introduced in the procedural modelling generation process before the placement of transitions: shape adaptation for inner divisions. This step accomplishes the transformation of the division's shape to fulfil the requirement that defines the number of bounding wall segments. Therefore, some segments may be added or deleted from the shape accordingly with the parameter that sets the divisions' wall segments. Note that at this stage, the floor plan is in 2D (ground level) and these segments represent non-extruded walls, i.e. they are only 2D ground marks for a future extrusion.

The first grammar rules parameter that is related with the division definition establishes the number of wall segments that will delimit each division (a wall segment is defined by two consecutive points, before the extrusion step). This parameter is considered at the procedural modelling stage, after the division process. Thus, when the process of dividing the building's constraint polygon is complete—through the splitting operations guided by the treemap implicitly defined in rules—the resulting divisions are geometrically moulded by the exterior walls, while the wall segments that constitute a frontier with adjacent divisions maintain their format (which was

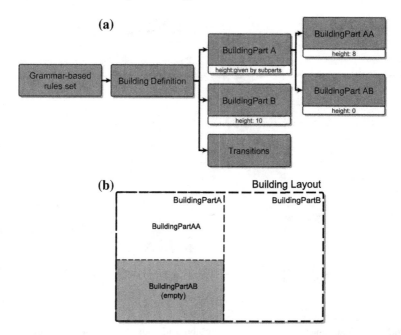

Fig. 6.1 Example of the fake-concave technique behaviour. In **a** is a graphical interpretation of the building parts specification (provided by definition rules). Each one of those building parts can be defined as a geometric hole if the height is set to 0. In **b** the expected result obtained from previous definition is presented. *BuildingPartAB* is a geometric hole because its height was set to 0, at the definition time

given by the initial splitting area created during the floor plan division stage). To match the number of each division's wall segments with the correspondent wall segments parameter value specified by the definition rules, some adjustments might have to occur, which means that some wall segments need to be added or subtracted to divisions that do not comply with the rules regarding the number of wall segments. These two adjustment processes are now described in greater detail.

(A) Adding wall segments to a division: while the number of wall segments belonging to a given division is lesser than the value defined in the rules, some operations have to be iteratively performed to increase the effective number of wall segments. These operations consist in testing and finding the most longer segment to be replaced by a certain point, avoiding interfering with inner transitions. Thereby, at the beginning of the process, a simulation to place those transitions is performed (preliminary step with no effective changes). Afterwards, each point of the division shape (formed by its segment walls) is subjected to an isolated simulation (for a given iteration, all other points remain in the shape while a particular point is exclusively tested). Each simulation consists in the replacement of a selected point by a segment formed by two other points, properly spaced between the former and its next point and also between the former and

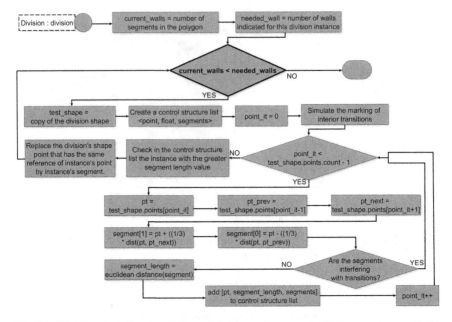

Fig. 6.2 Workflow depicting the addition of division wall segments. Wall segments are added to the existing division wall, while the number of division wall segments is lesser than required. Each iteration avoids interfering with interior transitions and uses the most lengthy segment to increase the wall, which aims a balanced distribution of segments throughout the wall

its previous point, more specifically, at $1/3$ of each one. As long as that segment does not collide with transition marks, the length of the replacing segment is calculated and stored along with the testing point in a dynamic structure. Otherwise, the segment is ignored and the process continues to the next point. After testing all points belonging to the division's shape, the aforementioned structure is traversed to check the segment with the greater length and the effective replacement occurs in the associated point. The process is repeated until the effective number of wall segments comply with the rules. The wall segments addition workflow is presented in the Fig. 6.2.

(B) Deleting wall segments from a division: alternatively, if a given division exceeds the required number of wall segments—specified by the rules—then one or more segments need to be deleted without interfering with transitions. Thus, initially, a simulation is performed to place the division's transitions, temporarily (preliminary step with no effective changes). The set of points constituting the shape formed by the division's wall segments are subjected to a test that aims to find the candidate point for exclusion, involving the minimal division area loss. Thereby, for each point, the following set of operations are carried out: first, the point is selected; then, the point is temporarily removed from the aforementioned shape; a verification is also made to ascertain if there are any transition affected by that removal; if so, the current point is ignored and the

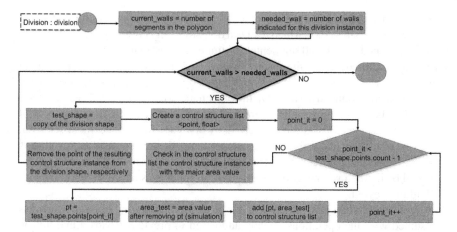

Fig. 6.3 Workflow depicting the operations regarding the deletion of a division's wall segments. While the number of wall segments is higher than required, wall segments are taken out (through point elimination) in an operation that ensures the minimal waste of a division's area

next one is processed from the first step; otherwise, the process continues with shape's area being calculated and associated to this point; finally, the removed point is restored. When the testing process is ended for all points, the one having the associated higher area value is effectively removed, reflecting this change in the wall segments. The process is applied while the number of wall segments is greater than the specified by definition rules seeking, in each iteration, the preservation of the widest division's area as possible. Figure 6.3 depicts the general workflow for the division's wall segments removal.

The process of division walls adaptation (addition or deletion of points) also relies in the following assumptions:

- The maximum number of division wall segments is 8. When the rules provide a higher value than 8, the value 8 is considered instead of the defined. Although higher limiting values do not seem to represent a problematic issue for the effectiveness of this procedural modelling methodology, the established limit of 8 wall segments foresees to restrain the computational burden. Besides, this value seems reasonable to demonstrate the goal of the process that regards wall adaptation;
- The minimum number of wall segments is 4. If the defined number of division walls provided by rules is lower than 4, it is overwritten to the referred minimum value. The value 4 was defined to ensure that all of the connecting divisions maintain their adjacent wall segments to support transitions, even in the most demanding scenarios (for example, the case of a central division surrounded by other connecting divisions, in which each wall segment belonging to that central division is in contact with a room, at least);
- If the value 0 is provided, the adjustment step for division wall is ignored for the respective division.

Some considerations about the worst case scenario on each operation regarding wall adaptation need to be clarified. Central divisions fully connected with all neighbours and shaped with 4 wall segments constitute the most demanding case when the 8 walls are required by definition rules. In this case, a lack of space compromising transitions placement prevents a well-distributed operation regarding wall segments addition, causing rounded corners. On the other hand, a division placed near at one of the building layout margins, at its centre, and requiring the minimum number of wall segments (4 segments) would constitute the worst case for wall segment removal. Due to the restriction of 4 wall segments at minimum, the inner transitions are always ensured. However, requirements regarding entry doors (access to the building exterior) will be ignored whenever divisions in those conditions lose the adjacency with the building layout.

After wall segments adaptation stage, the procedural modelling generation process is resumed with the operations already addressed in previous Chaps. 4 and 5. The division graph, already specified by the ontology-based grammar (definition) rules and now loaded into an ontology-based class set is used to place the transition doors between connecting divisions. Afterwards, windows and entry doors are properly placed in the virtual building layout limits.

A last set of operations involving extrusions then takes place to attain the 3D virtual building model. So, the walls are extruded considering the aforementioned transitions. Finally, grounds and ceilings, roofs are produced along with some building completions that aim to enhance the 3D model with details.

6.1.4 Stochastic Rules Selection for the Automatic Generation of Virtual Buildings

The stochastic process that is about to be presented aims to constitute a preliminary and experimental mechanism for the random production of virtual buildings, thus providing a modest but reliable alternative for automating the production of buildings using the addressed procedural modelling methodology. There are two approaches for stochastic generation: one for producing random virtual buildings with a desired division set and building configuration in which a list of divisions has to be provided along with the required configuration as input; and other to generate a set of random buildings (with random configurations) with aleatory divisions' sets in which the number of buildings to be generated is the only parameter needed. After being provided with the proper minimal parameters, both approaches ensure a fully automatic generation process based on interrelated node graphs.

The selections involved on the former approach are made considering a given divisions' list that gathers priority-one and priority-two divisions (provided as input) and also a building configuration (ranging L-shaped, U-shaped or convex). This approach starts by isolating priority-one and priority-two divisions in two different lists. Then, priority-one divisions are picked up: they can be social (e.g. living rooms)

or service oriented (e.g. kitchens). The selection relies on a pseudorandom generation number approach ranging the list of priority-one divisions. By convention,
those divisions are set as entry rooms that provide access to the virtual building's
exterior. The first layer graph is automatically composed with the selected priority-
one division nodes which are set to be interconnected (a node connection implies
a connection between associated divisions which will have a common transition).
Moreover, a set of marginal nodes representing the boundaries of those priority-one
divisions are created and categorized as top, bottom, left or right. The only exception
regards the contacting margins of the priority-one divisions which need to be unob-
structed to allow the interconnectivity of those divisions. For example, considering
two priority-one division nodes with a side-by-side disposition, the right margin of
the left node and the left margin of the right node are not created to enable the
aforementioned connection between those divisions. Such margins can be seen as
temporary nodes—representing temporary containers—for arrangement purposes.
Furthermore, there is a second step that consists in mounting the second layer graph
of division nodes. Towards this goal, priority-two divisions (i.e. private rooms such
as bedrooms and toilets) are consecutively picked from their list using a pseudorandom number generator. Each randomly selected priority-two division is converted
to a node and associated to a priority-one division margin. A pseudorandom number generator is used once again in two phases, one for attributing a priority-one
division node and other for selecting its margin. The second layer graph is considered completed when all the priority-two division nodes have an associated margin
belonging to a particular priority-one division node. Then, some nodes representing
corridors might be attached between the divisions belonging to both layers to ensure a
fully connectable floor plan definition or, in other words, to avoid isolated divisions
(for example, a corridor node has to be placed between a marginal bathroom and
a priority-one kitchen to avoid the isolation of that bathroom, since those division
types are not directly connectable). A simplified scheme depicting the aforementioned main steps is presented in Fig. 6.4. Finally, the requirements regarding the
building configuration must be satisfied. The following topics will expose the three
supported configurations along with the process actions to achieve a valid definition
for each case.

- Convex configuration: the process does not make any alteration to the node-based
  structure which stays as-is;
- L-shaped configuration: a special node marked as empty is added to one of the
  extreme nodes representing a priority-one division. Thus, during the node-based
  structure conversion into ontology-based rules, that priority-one division node
  holding the special empty node is unfolded in two building parts rules: one defining
  a disposable building part at the building corner and other properly loaded with
  the specifications of the priority-one division node (the carrier);
- U-shaped configuration: to achieve that one, a new priority-one division node has
  to be created with a corridor node and a special empty node. Then, that node is
  attached between two consecutive priority-one division nodes while their connections are properly adapted to link to the corridor within this new node. By this

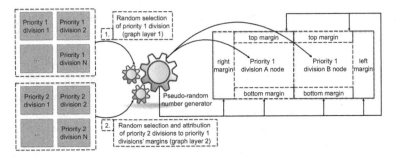

Fig. 6.4 Simplified scheme of the stochastic process, depicting the main steps regarding the random selection and arrangement of both priority-one and priority-two divisions. For a given division list (provided as input or stochastically determined) priority-one and priority-two divisions are separated in two distinct sub-lists. Then, priority-one divisions are randomly selected and interconnected and, for each one, nodes representing margins are attached (the contacting sides belonging to different connecting priority-one nodes are not provided with such margin nodes to avoid future conflicts regarding the placement of transitions). Finally, priority-two divisions are randomly selected and distributed by the previously created margins belonging to priority-one divisions. Configurations regarding the building format are not addressed in this scheme

way, it is achieved the intention of defining a disposable building part in the middle of a building's margin to form the U-shape (or some similar variant), during the conversion of the node-based structure into grammar-based rules.

It is noteworthy that the use of different area levels, specifically room priorities and double-level layer graphs, is based on the suggestions left by Lopes et al. [10] and Marson and Musse [11].

The latter stochastic approach—that only requires the number of virtual buildings to be produced as an input—has an additional starting step that relies on specifying rooms' list and building's configuration, for each building to be generated. Thus, a set of pseudorandom number generations selects one or two priority-one divisions namely a kitchen and or a living room (a division extension created for the stochastic process). Then, priority-two divisions are selected. For each type, specifically private rooms and bathrooms, a random number is generated to determine the number of type instances that will integrate the list being created (e.g. if the pseudorandom generator retrieves the number 6 for private rooms then the reference for this room type is added six times to the divisions list under construction). When the division list is completed, a random building configuration is automatically chosen from the supported formats (L-shaped, U-shaped and convex). Afterwards, the previously described stochastic approach is applied to randomly arrange those rooms in a double-layer graph-based structure.

After obtaining the graph-based structure representing divisions' arrangements and connections, these structural definitions are transformed into ontology-based grammar rules for the application of the aforementioned process moderation process, followed by the procedural modelling process responsible for creating the virtual building model. This is valid for both stochastic approaches.

It should be emphasized that the defined stochastic process is not concerned with real-world architectural rules. It only constitutes a process for the random virtual building generation that aims to overcome the deterministic nature of the treemap approach adopted for this procedural modelling methodology.

6.2 Final Procedural Modelling Methodology Implementation

A software system integrating two tools—deterministic and stochastic—was developed to support virtual buildings generation using this final procedural modelling methodology version. The deterministic tool relies on a graphical user interface (GUI) that allows to draw the desired floor plans and to parametrize each operation. Regarding the stochastic tool, it produces random virtual buildings, considering high-level requirements. Both tools are depicted in Fig. 6.5.

Besides the aforementioned tools, the software toolkit also integrates a backoffice that enables the user to adjust default parameters. Such parameters map the restriction rules identified on Chap. 5 and are used by the procedural modelling implementation in strategic steps of a building generation. Thus, one can modify the textures of the different elements (e.g. doors, walls, windows, roof) and the values associated with the construction of the models and geometrical operations (e.g. the definition of door occupation in a wall segment, weight attribution for the reserved grammatical words "big", "medium" and "small" wall thickness). These possibilities allow the customization of the final models and partial control of the modeller's behaviour.

The stochastic and deterministic tools that make part of this toolkit will be detailed in the next subsections.

6.2.1 Deterministic Tool

To rapidly create virtual building models while ensuring a certain level of step-by-step control by the user, a parametric tool was developed (Fig. 6.5, bottom). This tool is capable of generating grammatical rules through a small number of user interactions. The user starts by defining the building's shape (its outline contour). Then, a set of building parts must be specified. These building parts can also be subdivided into other building parts for arrangement purposes. If a building part is divided in the horizontal orientation, then subsequent containers inside of it will produce vertically arranged building parts. According to the defined grammar, this parametric tool requests the roof type and the building part height, through a graphical prompt window opportunely presented to allow the parametrization of a building parts. A height defined with a value of 0 specifies a disposable part (such building parts are removed right after the floor plan division stage foreseeing the creation of building

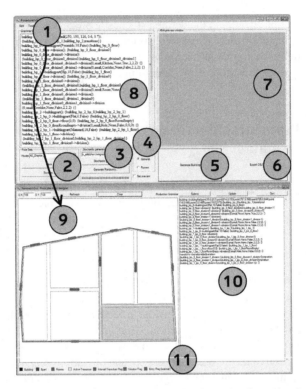

Fig. 6.5 Screenshot of the procedural modelling system implementing the stochastic and parametric tools. The upper part of the figure depicts the main GUI, which is composed of the following: (*1*) access to the deterministic parametric tool; (*2*) a file area to manage the stored grammatical rules; (*3*) a stochastic menu area that allows the user to rapidly generate a building with a specific list of divisions or even a set of random buildings; (*4*) the style, which can be general or roman; (*5*) a button to request the generation of a building regarding the grammatical rules contained in (*8*); (*6*) a button to export the building in wavefront obj format; (*7*) the XNA floor plan previewer; and (*8*) a grammatical rules area. The lower part of the image presents the deterministic parametric tool: (*9*) the floor plan drawing area with several colours to help distinguish the input elements; (*10*) an area that presents the grammatical rules during user drawings and parametrization; and (*11*) captions for the colours used to identify the drawn elements

layouts with holes and/or non-convex configurations). Then, divisions can be integrated inside the building parts. Through mouse clicking, the user can populate a building part with divisions (rooms). Once again, division arrangement is allowed through the definition of final divisions inside division containers. The division direction behaves similarly to that which was explained for building parts: divisions are arranged vertically if the container has a horizontal orientation, and vice versa. The parametric tool asks for the set of parameters that should define a given division, such as the number of delimiting walls, division type, number of windows, internal structure and flag for entry doors (transitions interfacing the building exterior), using a prompt window as it occurs in building parts parametrization. The tool also supports the easy definition of division connectivity. The simple act of right clicking upon the starting division and selecting the target division for connection is sufficient to generate the rule that relates them in terms of transitions.

It is also important to stress out that the tool asks for parameters according to the operation's context. For example, if a division is being defined, then only the required division parameters are asked to comply with the proper grammatical rule. This is helpful in reducing malformed grammatical rules, which could result in incoherent models.

6.2.2 Stochastic Tool

The manageable and flexible nature of the treemap approach allowed the development of a semi-/fully automatic tool (Fig. 6.5, top) that implements a process capable of producing random virtual buildings.

As input, the tool accepts a divisions list which has to be selected by the user through a combo box control (Fig. 6.5, circle 3) that contains a preloaded set of division lists in the following format:

```
building_name(room0, room1, ..., roomN)[configuration]
```

The selected divisions are then divided into a couple of lists, accordingly with their priorities. Afterwards, priority-one divisions (kitchens or living rooms) are selected and connected and some marginal areas are also attached to each division (avoiding interference with the referred connection). Then, priority-two divisions are related to priority-one divisions' margins using pseudorandom attributions and some corridors are created to ensure connectivity between those two categories of rooms. The process results in a hierarchical node-based structure. The last field—configuration—refers to the building's configuration and intends to provide the possibility of producing L-shaped, U-shaped or fully convex buildings, on demand. L-shaped or U-shaped configurations require the integration of a node representing a disposable building part. Such node is strategically attached to the previously determined node-based structure to properly define an empty building part for one of the building's corners (L-shape case) or at the centre of one of its margins (U-shape case).

Alternatively, the user can produce a set of virtual buildings based on a unique input: the desired number of buildings to be produced (Fig. 6.5, circle 3, second button). After that, an iterative and automatic process to produce the required number of buildings is started, and two main tasks are executed for each building. The first one is responsible for the pseudorandom selection of a divisions list, for each building to be generated. The following conditions affect each list selection: there can be one or two priority-one divisions; the number of private divisions cannot exceed nine; the number of bathrooms cannot overcome the number of private rooms. Next, a building configuration is also randomly picked from the following available set: L-shape, U-shape or convex. Afterwards, the second task takes place accordingly to which was already explained in the previous paragraph. The process executes until the number of generated rooms complies the user requirements.

The outputs of these tools are ontology-based grammar rules that are forced to pass through a pair of built-in modules aiming the generation of the final virtual building model (similarly to the system presented on Chap. 5): the rules moderation module and procedural generation module. The first module validates the grammar-based definition rules, loads an ontology-based class set and ensures the feasibility of the floor plan through a probing process. Then, the class set is submitted to the procedural generation module which applies a set of steps—included in the main stages responsible for the effective floor plan production, building extrusions and also building completions—to achieve the final form of the 3D building model.

6.3 Preliminary Tests and Results

A set of structures was produced using the presented deterministic tool that implements the latest procedural modelling methodology features. Figure 6.6 provides a first insight about the capabilities of the methodology's last version in generating different kinds of traversable buildings, in particular one constrained by a pure convex shape, another one exposing the results of the fake-concave strategy application and a last building depicting the wall's adaptation results regarding interior divisions.

An experiment was also carried out to demonstrate the applicability of the stochastic approach, through its homologous tool. Thus, a set of L-shaped buildings was produced considering the same set of divisions: a kitchen, a living room and three rooms. As it is depicted in Fig. 6.7, for each generation the referred set of divisions

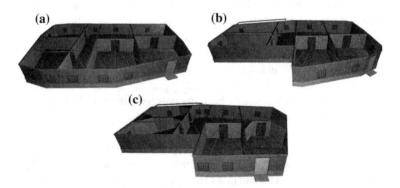

Fig. 6.6 Preliminary results depicting the traversable buildings generated with the final methodology: **a** shows a traversable building constrained by a pure convex polygon and composed by three connected corridors, a kitchen, a bathroom and two bedrooms; **b** and **c** have a similar configuration, being both constrained by non-convex polygons due to the fake-concave technique; **c** also presents the results of a inner wall definition for the geometric adaptation of inner divisions

Fig. 6.7 Preliminary results of the stochastic approach: five generations were made using the same set of rooms (divisions)—a kitchen a living room and three rooms. The result is a set of L-shape buildings that hold the same set of divisions but with random arrangements

is maintained but their organization is randomly altered. Corridors are also created, in some cases, to ensure the connectivity between all inner divisions.

6.4 Summary

This chapter presented a semi-automatic methodology capable of producing 3D buildings constrained by arbitrary shapes in which the generation process is guided by sets of grammar rules, that resulted from the definition of an abstract ontology for describing buildings generically. This version of the methodology supports the definition of building constraints which can be geometrically convex or not, due to fake-concave technique. Moreover, the wall segments of the interior divisions can also be altered accordingly with the grammar rules to modify divisions' geometry. A stochastic process was also engaged with the final procedural modelling methodology to enable the automatic generation of random buildings. In short, a set of divisions or a desired number of structures to be generated are provided as input to trigger a randomized generation of virtual buildings.

Also, a system implementation regarding the final methodology version was presented with two tools: a deterministic tool that enables handmade floor plan drawings and parametrizations and a stochastic tool capable of producing random buildings with low user interaction. The former makes a progressive definition of ontology-based grammar rules while the user is drawing and parametrizing the desired floor plan. The latter autonomously produces a double-layer division graph that is converted into grammar rules. Two types of inputs in the form of simple parameters are sufficient to trigger the action of this second tool: a list of divisions or a number of virtual buildings to be generated.

To accomplish the virtual building generation task, the grammar-based rules (also known as definition rules) produced by both of the aforementioned tools are verified by the rules moderation module and, after proper validation, they are forwarded to the procedural modelling module which is responsible for producing the 3D virtual building enhanced with some details like inner footers and stair steps for entry doors.

The preliminary tests provide a first insight about the capabilities of both methodology and stochastic process. However, an extended set of results will be presented in the next chapter which is reserved for the evaluation of the final procedural modelling methodology version.

References

1. Rau-Chaplin, A., MacKay-Lyons, B., Spierenburg, P.: The Lahave house project: towards and automated architectural design service. In: Proceedings of the International Conference on Computer Aided Design (CADEX-96), pp. 62–66. IEEE (1996)
2. Wonka, P., Wimmer, M., Sillion, F., Ribarsky, W.: Instant architecture. ACM Trans. Graph. **22**(3), 669–677 (2003). ISSN 0730-0301. doi:10.1145/882262.882324
3. Larive, M., Gaildrat, V.: Wall grammar for building generation. In: Proceedings of the 4th International Conference on Computer Graphics and Interactive Techniques in Australasia and Southeast Asia, GRAPHITE '06, pp. 429–437, New York, NY, USA, 2006. ACM (2006). ISBN 1-59593-564-9. doi:10.1145/1174429.1174501
4. Müller, P., Wonka, P., Haegler, S., Ulmer, A., Van Gool, L.: Procedural modeling of buildings. ACM Trans. Graph. **25**(3), 614–623 (2006). ISSN 0730-0301. doi:10.1145/1141911.1141931
5. Rodrigues, N., Gonzaga Magalhães, L., Paulo Moura, J., Chalmers, A.: Automatic reconstruction of virtual heritage sites. In: Proceedings of the 9th International Conference on Virtual Reality, Archaeology and Cultural Heritage, pp. 39–46. Eurographics Association (2008)
6. Hohmann, B., Havemann, S., Krispel, U., Fellner, D.: A GML shape grammar for semantically enriched 3d building models. Comput. Graph. **34**(4), 322–334 (2010). ISSN 0097-8493. doi:10.1016/j.cag.2010.05.007. http://www.sciencedirect.com/science/article/pii/S0097849310000749. Procedural Methods in Computer Graphics Illustrative Visualization
7. Trescak, T., Esteva, M., Rodriguez, I.: A virtual world grammar for automatic generation of virtual worlds. Vis. Comput. **26**(6–8), 521–531 (2010). ISSN 0178-2789. doi:10.1007/s00371-010-0473-7
8. Lindenmayer, A.: Mathematical models for cellular interactions in development ii. simple and branching filaments with two-sided inputs. J. Theor. Biol. **18**(3), 300–315 (1968). ISSN 0022-5193. doi:10.1016/0022-5193(68)90080-5. http://www.sciencedirect.com/science/article/pii/0022519368900805
9. Johnson, B., Shneiderman, B.: Treemaps: a space-filling approach to the visualization of hierarchical information structures. In: Proceedings of the IEEE Conference on Visualization, 1991, Visualization'91, pp. 284–291. IEEE (1991)
10. Lopes, R., Tim, T., Smelik, R.M., de Kraker, K.J., Bidarra, R.: A constrained growth method for procedural floor plan generation. In: GAMEON'10, November (2010). http://graphics.tudelft.nl/~rafa/myPapers/bidarra.GAMEON10.pdf
11. Marson, F., Raupp Musse, S.: Automatic real-time generation of floor plans based on squarified treemaps algorithm. Int. J. Comput. Games Technol. **2010**, 7:1–7:10 (2010). ISSN 1687-7047. doi:10.1155/2010/624817

Chapter 7
Procedural Modelling Methodology Evaluation

Abstract The evaluation of the presented procedural modelling methodology will be addressed in this chapter. Thus, a set of tests made to demonstrate the capabilities of this methodology in producing buildings compliant with a real subset of architectural rules (RGEU [1]) and others with distinct formats and different architectonic structures will be presented. Moreover, the effectiveness of the treemap approach in subdividing random layouts is shown, along with a generic stochastic process for automatic building generation and also some computational performance measurements that point out to the methodology expeditiousness.

7.1 Towards the Compliance of Real-World Architectonic Rules

The virtual buildings that are produced for areas like architecture or archaeology are expected to be convincing and faithful while ensuring concordance with a specific architectonic style that is outlined by a given set of structural guidelines or rules. To attend this issue and considering that there is a large diversity of architectonic styles, both the planning and the development stages of the presented procedural modelling methodology were carried out considering features such as abstractness and flexibility foreseeing, simultaneously, its adaptation to distinct architectural requirements with the least possible changes to the source code. In fact, to enable those code-independent adaptations, a clear separation was made between parameters (input or default rules) and the implementation details. In this section, two examples of houses complaint with some RGEU [1] rules—the portuguese regulation for urban edifications—will be provided. Thereby, some requirements belonging to that regulation will be presented and, then, the respective houses fulfilling such requirements will be shown as a result of the adaptation of parameters regarding the procedural modelling tool defaults and the user-based rules.

© The Author(s) 2016
T. Adão et al., *Ontology-based Procedural Modelling of Traversable Buildings Composed by Arbitrary Shapes*, SpringerBriefs in Computer Science, DOI 10.1007/978-3-319-42372-2_7

7.1.1 RGEU Rules

Some RGEU rules establishing legal requirements for the construction of buildings in Portugal were considered for this demonstration which intends to highlight the flexibility of the procedural modelling methodology in adapting real-world architectonic rules.

- Room and building minimum areas (66.° and 67.° articles): RGEU rules impose a minimum area for rooms and buildings, according to the building typology. For instance, a T2 building must have a minimum area of $72\,m^2$. In turn, each double room, living room and kitchen must have, at least and, respectively, 9, 12, $6\,m^2$. By convenience, double rooms will be simply identified as bedrooms in this particular section;
- Rules for toilets (68.° and 86.° articles): RGEU establishes that the minimum size of a T2 toilet is $3.5\,m^2$. Moreover, connections between toilets and other building compartments—such as a dining room or a kitchen—are not recommended, except in some specific situations;
- Transversal ventilation (72.° article): The ventilation of a building must be ensured, preferably, through the placement of windows in two opposite facades, according to RGEU rules;
- Courtyard protection against water infiltration (76.° article): Building outdoor spaces must have some kind of water infiltration protection such as a strip. This element should be complemented by a condign space such as a garden area, as it is suggested in RGEU.

7.1.2 Examples of T2 Houses in Compliance with RGEU Rules

A couple of T2 houses were produced by the procedural modelling methodology toolkit which was configured to support the aforementioned RGEU rules. Thereby, using the toolkit's backoffice, some restriction rules regarding rooms' dimensions were properly altered, as it is presented below:

- Parameter "small": growth proportion that was set up to 1. Kitchen's size was used as reference;
- Parameter "medium": growth proportion that was set up to 1.5. This attribution was made considering that medium rooms (i.e. double rooms) are 1.5 times bigger than the smallest ones;
- Parameter "big": growth proportion that was set up to 2. This attribution was made considering that big rooms (i.e. living rooms) are twice as bigger as the smallest ones;
- Parameters to restrict borrowing: since some space borrowings might occur during the floor plan division, as it was explained earlier in this book, there are some

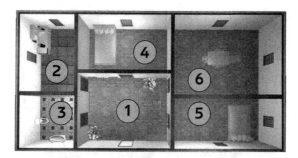

Fig. 7.1 T2 house with 72 m^2 complying with RGEU rules. It contains six rooms: a corridor (*1*) with several door passages that lead to a kitchen (*2*) with an area of 12 m^2, to a toilet (*3*) measuring 6 m^2, to a couple of bedrooms (*4* and *5*) each one with 11 m^2 and also to a living room (*6*) occupying 18 m^2. Transversal ventilation is ensured by the windows placed in kitchen (*2*) and living room (*6*) or in the living room (*6*) and bedroom 5, for example

parameters that aim to avoid undersized rooms phenomena by restricting that borrowing. Those parameters force small, medium and big rooms to maintain their areas higher than 6, 9 and 12 m^2, respectively, during the borrowing steps.

In addition, two sets of definition rules were produced to represent a couple of T2 houses, one of them having a garden. A scale relation of 10 pixels to 1 m was adopted to manage areas. Some furniture[1] was manually placed inside both the houses to improve the intuitiveness of the reader. Those houses comply with RGEU rules and will be presented next:

(A) Simple T2 house: the first T2 house (Fig. 7.1) is composed by a corridor connecting the rest of its divisions, more specifically, a kitchen, two bedrooms, a living room and a toilet. This T2 house complies with the four RGEU rules previously presented. The footprint of the building has 72 m^2 whilst the kitchen, both of the bedrooms and living room occupy an area of 12, 11 m^2 (each) and 18 m^2, respectively. Transversal ventilation is ensured in all of the opposite facades. Finally, the toilet access was made available through the referred corridor, to comply with the RGEU rule about toilets' connectivity. Toilet's area is around 6 m^2 (larger than the minimum required, that is, 3.5 m^2).

(B) Simple T2 house with garden: a second T2 house with an exterior backyard (Fig. 7.2) was designed, using the presented procedural modelling methodology. Just like the first house, a transversal entry corridor ensures access to the remaining divisions, i.e. a kitchen, a toilet, a couple of bedrooms a living room and also a garden. This house is also respecting the aforementioned RGEU recommendations. Regarding areas, both interior and exterior components are in conformity: the building footprint has 84 m^2 while the interior kitchen and

---

[1]The procedurally generated T2 houses compliant with some RGEU rules were equipped with some virtual furniture, available for free download and use in the TurboSquid website. For more information, please, check the link http://www.turbosquid.com/.

(a)

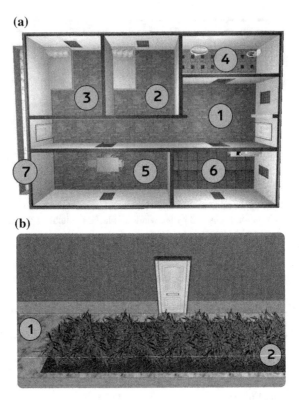

(b)

Fig. 7.2 T2 house with an area of 84 m² and a garden, complying with RGEU rules: **a** depicts the top view of a building that is composed by a couple of merged corridors (*a-1*) that leads to a pair of individual bedrooms (*a-2* and *a-3*) each one measuring 13 m², to a toilet (*a-4*) with 8.5 m², to a living room (*a-5*) occupying 12.9 m² and also to a kitchen (*a-6*) with an area of 13 m². House's garden (*a-7*) fills the remaining area; **b** gives particular focus to that garden which has an ambulatory space (*b-1*), a strip wall and a central gardening area (*b-2*). Transversal ventilation is ensured by some windows strategically placed in rooms leaning against opposite facades, for example, the ones depicted by *a-2* and *a-5*

both of the bedrooms occupy 13 m², a value only surpassed by the living room that occupies 17 m². Traversable ventilation is also ensured through a couple of opposite facades. Building's toilet has an area of 8.5 m² which is greater than the minimum required (3.5 m²) and its access is only available through the corridor. At last, the house garden has an ambulatory space and a wall strip to avoid water infiltration and, at its centre, there is a gardening zone.

Other pertinent example of the presented procedural modelling methodology adaptation to other architectonic styles will be shown later in this section with a *domus* composed by an *atrium* and a *peristylium*, considering some of the requirements pointed out by Rodrigues [2] for a typical Roman house.

Despite the potential usefulness of this procedural modelling methodology to areas such as architecture or archaeology, it is undeniable that another layer to control and validate the input parameters against real-world laws is still needed to allow a proper adaptation of different architectonic styles.

7.2 Virtual Buildings Constrained by Arbitrary Shapes

Tests were performed to validate the methodology addressed in this book, while generating simple buildings based on the generic ontology. Thereby, a set of virtual models are presented to show the coarse generation of 3D buildings constrained by a convex polygon or by a fake-concave technique-based shape. All of them were produced respecting the limits of a convex polygon randomly outlined by a convex hull generator method. A description of each one is presented bellow:

(A) Simple building model convexly constrained:
 The simplest building is constrained by a convex polygon and composed of a room, a kitchen, a toilet and a central corridor connecting all of the other divisions. The following grammar-based rules create the virtual building depicted in Fig. 7.3a;
(B) U-shaped building model:
 An U-shaped building takes advantage of the already referred fake-concave technique. The virtual building consists of a kitchen, that provides access to the building and connects to a living room (big division), that in turn interfaces with a room and a bathroom. The next grammar-based rules exemplify the generation of this type of buildings and the result is depicted in Fig. 7.3b;
(C) L-shaped building model:
 An L-shaped building also takes advantage of the already referred fake-concave strategy. The building consists of a kitchen, two side rooms and two connected central divisions ensuring that all other divisions are reachable. Figure 7.3c depicts the modelling result;
(D) L-shaped building model (more complex):
 A second L-shaped building—a little more complex—is constrained by a random convex polygon that contains several rooms, a toilet and also an entry kitchen (Fig. 7.3d). A central corridor connects to a couple of rooms, a bathroom and also interfaces with two corridors. One of these corridors provides access to the house and the other one connects to an entry kitchen, a smaller bathroom and also to a small room. These corridors are not connected by transition doors. Instead, the procedural modelling system creates a doorless transition to connect them.

The set of tests was posteriorly extended to demonstrate the effectiveness of the division wall adaptation process.

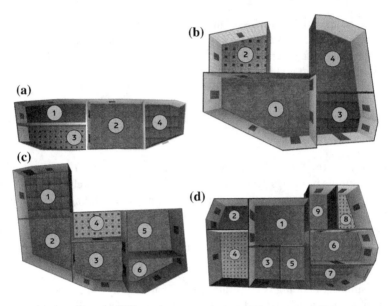

Fig. 7.3 Set of virtual buildings based on the generic ontology and constrained by arbitrary layouts, generated through the procedural modelling methodology: **a** depicts the simplest building of this demonstration with a room (*1*), a central hall passage (*2*), a bathroom (*3*) and a kitchen (*4*); in **b** there is a U-shaped building, with an entry room (*1*) that connects with a bathroom (*2*), a kitchen (*3*) and a private room(*4*); **c** presents an L-shaped building with an entry kitchen (*1*), two connected rooms acting as hall passages (*2*, *3*), one of them interfacing with toilet (*4*) and two private rooms (*5*, *6*); finally, **d** shows a building with three corridors connected through doorless transitions in which the central corridor (*1*) connects to a couple of private rooms (*2*, *3*), a bathroom (*4*), an entry corridor (*5*) and lateral hallway (*6*) that, in turn, interfaces with a kitchen (*7*), another private room (*9*) and a small bathroom (*8*)

7.3 Interior Divisions' Walls Adaptation

A process for inner wall adaptation was established and described in Chap. 6. This subsection intends to present the variety of structures that this methodology is capable of generating using the referred method and also considering the holes provided by the fake-concave technique. Next, each one of those structures will be addressed:

(A) L-shaped building model (six divisions):
   The building model depicted in Fig. 7.4a has an entry kitchen formed by 7 inner wall segments. The kitchen interfaces with a flattened long corridor, composed by 6 inner wall segments, that connects to a central hall also with 6 wall segments. This corridor also connects to another corridor composed by 5 wall segments, that, in turn, connects to a couple of divisions: a bathroom with 6 wall segments and a room with 5 wall segments.

(B) L-shaped building model (nine divisions):
   This building model has an entry kitchen with no adaptation required (0 wall

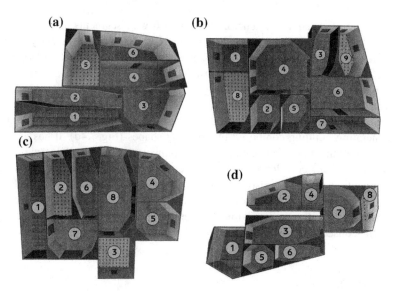

Fig. 7.4 Set of virtual buildings constrained by arbitrary layouts and containing divisions with adapted inner walls, generated through the procedural modelling methodology: **a** depicts an L-shaped building that has a set of connected divisions including a kitchen with 7 wall segments (*1*), two corridors composed by a 6-segment wall (*2, 3*), a third corridor composed by a 5-segment wall (*4*), a bathroom (*5*) and a private room (*6*) with 6 and 5 wall segments, respectively; **b** depicts another L-shaped building composed by a set of three rooms (*1, 2, 3*) delimited by 5, 6 and 8 wall segments, three corridors (*4, 5, 6*) with 6, 7 and 0 wall segments (0 is the value that defines that the division's wall segments remain unchanged), a kitchen (*7*) without wall adaptation (0 wall segments) and two bathrooms (*8, 9*), both with 6 wall segments; in **c** there is a T-shaped building containing a kitchen (*1*) with 4 walls, two bathrooms (*2, 3*), one having 5 wall segments and other without segment restriction, three private rooms (*4, 5, 6*) each one containing 6 wall segments and a couple of connected corridors (*7, 8*) surrounded by 7 and 8 wall segments, respectively; finally **d** shows a building model composed by a kitchen (*1*) and a room (*2*) with 5 wall segments each, a couple of corridors (*3, 4*) both constrained by 6 wall segments, a couple of rooms (*5, 6*) with 7 wall segments each, yet another corridor (*7*) having 8 wall segments and a bathroom with 6 wall segments (*8*)

segments), that connects to a side corridor, also with 0 wall segments signalling that no adaptation is required. The corridor connects to a bathroom with 6 wall segments and to a room with 8 wall segments. It also interfaces with a big corridor containing 6 wall segments that allows traversing to a small entry corridor and to a room with 7 and 6 wall segments, respectively. Moreover, it provides access to another room with 5 wall segments and to a bathroom containing 6 wall segments. Figure 7.4b, depicts this building model.

(C) T-shaped building model:
Another building (Fig. 7.4c), identified as the third house, was generated regarding interior walls that form constraint n-gons to delimit inner divisions. This house is composed by an entry kitchen, forced to contain four wall segments, that connects to a corridor with 7 wall segments which in turn gives access to

a couple of divisions: a generic room with 6 wall segments and a bathroom surrounded by 5 wall segments. From it, there is also access to an entry room (8 wall segments) that interfaces with a couple of rooms, both with 7 wall segments and to a bathroom with no wall restrictions.

(D) Building model with a complex layout:

The last virtual building generated for this section is pretty unconventional, nevertheless, it intends to show the flexibility of the presented methodology in generating building composed by arbitrary shapes (Fig. 7.4d). It has an entry kitchen with 5 inner wall segments, that connects to a long corridor with 6 wall segments. This corridor, connects to a couple of rooms composed by 7 wall segments each. There is also a transition to another corridor constrained by 8 wall segments that interfaces with a bathroom and with yet another corridor, each one formed by 6 wall segments (almost imperceptible due to the similar orientations of the consecutive wall segments). Finally, this last corridor provides access to a room with 5 wall segments.

7.4 Subdivision Provided by the Treemap Approach

The adopted treemap approach was also tested to demonstrate floor plan's division process effectiveness and flexibility. The objective is to demonstrate that treemap is capable of producing more than nine divisions, outperforming the tests made in the last section. Thus, using grammar rules, four different structures were created with distinct morphologies and also division sets, all of them connected to each other to ensure that all divisions are reachable. The first model is constrained by a pure convex shape and contains only ten divisions. The second structure is a bit more complex and has 15 divisions and two holes formed by disposable building parts. The third virtual model is composed by three holes using fake-concave approach. It has 20 reachable inner divisions. The most complex model includes 30 divisions and four disposable building parts (based on the fake-concave technique), constituting the holes of the structure. Figure 7.5 depicts these four models.

7.5 Generating Structures Stochastically

Tests made using the stochastic process for the automatic generation of virtual buildings, described in Chap. 6, are presented in this section. Four groups of tests were made. The first set focused on the generation of buildings constrained by a convex shape without holes, while the second and the third sets demonstrate that the referred stochastic process can also be employed for the production of L- and U-shaped buildings, respectively. Moreover, the models of the first three groups of tests were generated considering two priority-one division nodes—a kitchen and a living room, that can be considered perfectly usual service/public divisions—and a fixed set of

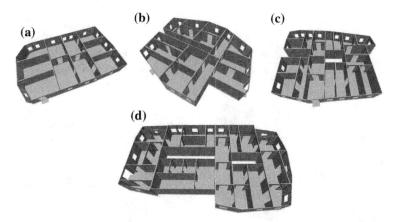

Fig. 7.5 Floor plan subdivision examples with four distinct structures: **a** exposes a structure with 10 divisions in a pure convex polygon. **b, c** and **d** depict fake-concave structures with 15, 20 and 30 divisions, respectively

priority-two division nodes, that were randomly distributed by the margins of the referred priority-one division nodes: three private rooms and one bathroom. The last set of virtual buildings enabled the fully automatic production of 3D buildings in a few minutes and with only a few inputs (a mouse click to demand the random genera-tion of buildings, a numeric value specifying the number of buildings to be generated and another mouse click to confirm). For each virtual building, a priority-one kitchen and a living room are selected with a random order, just like in the other testing sets. Then, a set of private rooms is randomly picked (one to nine in these tests). Also, a set of bathrooms is also selected with a restriction: its number cannot be higher than the number of private rooms. Both of the selected priority-one and priority-two division instances are integrated in a list. The building format (layout's constraint shape con-figuration) is randomly chosen from the following ones: fully convex, L-shaped or U-shaped. Next, a node set of priority-one and priority-two divisions is mounted as a treemap structure considering the previously selected divisions list and several oper-ations regarding pseudorandom selections and arrangements. The last step converts the graph and nodes into production grammar rules, that are passed to the procedural modelling module, responsible for the 3D model generation. Figure 7.6 depicts the results obtained using the stochastic process developed for the generation of random virtual buildings.

7.6 Ontology-Based Architectural Derivation

This section presents and demonstrates the buildings generation focusing the ontol-ogy derivation. To achieve it, some examples of structures extending from the generic ontology to represent elements belonging to the Roman architecture were used for

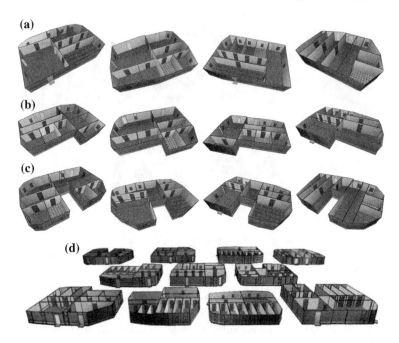

Fig. 7.6 Stochastic production of virtual buildings obtained from three fixed sets of divisions and a fourth set with randomly selected divisions. In **a**, **b** and **c** a fixed set of divisions—specifically a kitchen, a living room, three rooms and a bathroom—is used to generate several virtual buildings variants. While **a** depicts the possibilities of arrangements that can result from the referred divisions set inside a fully convex constraint polygon, **b** and **c** present the results with the same divisions set for L- and U-shaped houses, respectively. Finally, **d** exposes a subset of houses, taken from a group of 20 randomly generated buildings

concept proof purposes (both generic and Roman ontology were detailed in Chap. 3). Those structures were properly implemented in the procedural modelling module through a set of classes—following the object-oriented programming paradigm—that are used to guide the execution of the procedural modelling process. Furthermore, the geometrical definitions were also implemented for each one of those classes (instances of extension classes without geometric definitions make use of the geometry specified for their respective parent classes). Thus, it is possible to improve the procedural modelling module knowledge, based on the reuse of the generic ontology.

Specifically, a generic purpose building and a Roman *domus* that resulted from the aforementioned ontological extensions. The *domus* overrides the generic definitions to produce notably distinct structures such as *peristylium* gardens or *atrium* pools.

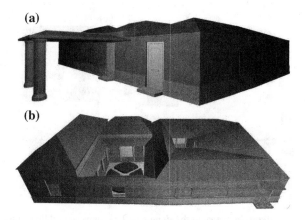

Fig. 7.7 Ontology-based generation of a generic building and a Roman *domus*. **a** Depicts a generic ontology-based building; **b** presents a Roman ontology-based *domus*. A part of its *peristylium* can be observed through the open roof with the widest aperture, at *domus* left side. The other open roof with the smallest aperture is the *compluvium* of the building's *atrium*

7.6.1 Generic Building and Roman **Domus** Overview

The generated virtual building (Fig. 7.7) that relies on the generic ontology has a set of divisions distributed by four building parts: an entry kitchen that connects to a small corridor which, in turn, leads to a central corridor that interfaces with other two small corridors: one corridor leads to a room and the other one interfaces with another room and also with another bathroom. Regarding the *domus* a typical Roman house-based structure was generated consisting of two main building parts: the *atrium* and the *peristylium*. The former has a water recoil system that consists of a sort of pool receiving water from a roof opening. The latter contains a big garden. Moreover, both the *atrium* and the *peristylium* can be seen as central corridors providing access to the majority of rooms inside the *domus*.

7.6.2 Structural Extensions and Differences

Several differences might be noticed in the structure of the generated buildings. The generic building has transitions enclosed by doors and windows bindings in opposition to the *domus*, that only contains openings in transitions. Both of these buildings contain a porch and a garden with distinct geometries and representations. The gardens of both buildings consist in open-air structures, but in the specific case of the *domus*, a garden is also a structure surrounded by columns that belongs to a *peristylium* division. Moreover, the generic building porch is supported by columns whereas the *domus* porch is not. Additionally, the *domus* was enriched with a special division called *atrium* to adapt a *compluvium/impluvium*. Therefore, the pro-

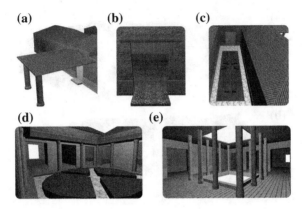

Fig. 7.8 Structural differences between the *domus* and the generic building: **a** and **b** depict the differences between the generic porch and the Roman porch; **c** and **d** expose the differences between the generic garden and the *peristylium* garden; finally **e** presents the *compluvium* and *impluvium* structures (used for water collection) that belong to the *domus atrium*

cedural modelling module was instructed to produce two structures in the presence of an *atrium* inside a building part: an *impluvium* that is a *Pool* extended from the *AbstractElement* of the generic ontology and a mansard roof with a central opening called *compluvium*. The textures were also changed to distinguish each architectonic structure. Figure 7.8 presents the aforementioned structures pointing out the main differences.

7.7 Performance Results

Performance tests were made to evaluate the impact of the methodology implementation in computer resources. The evaluation considered the following parameters: average load per CPU core, RAM usage, time and number of generated vertices. A computer equipped with an Intel[(R)] Core[(TM)] i7 CPU (model M620), at 2.67 GHz and 4 GB of RAM was used to perform this evaluation.

Specifically, the tests consisted in generating five groups of five virtual buildings each, with a gradual increment of building parts per group and divisions per generation. The first group has five generated virtual buildings with three, four, five, six and seven divisions organized in a single building part. The second one, contains five buildings with five, six, seven, eight and nine divisions distributed by two building parts. In the third group, five produced buildings composed by three building parts aggregating seven, eight, nine, ten and eleven divisions are presented. The penultimate set has five buildings, each one composed by four building parts that hold nine, ten, eleven, twelve and thirty divisions. Lastly, a set of five produced buildings are presented, each one having five building parts that are composed by eleven, twelve, thirteen, fourteen and fifteen divisions. The established inner transitions consisted in

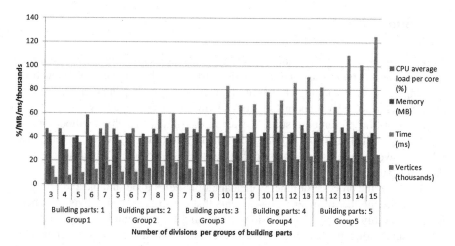

Fig. 7.9 Chart depicting the performance tests made to five groups of virtual buildings with a gradual increment of building parts per group and divisions per generation. *Group1* points out the performance results corresponding to the tests made with a single building part holding three, four, five, six and seven divisions; *Group2* presents the performance results considering two building parts containing five, six, seven, eight and nine divisions; the performance results regarding the generated buildings composed by three parts holding 7, 8, 9, 10 and 11 divisions are exposed in *Group3*; the fourth group (*Group4*) contains the performance results obtained by several configurations of four building parts containing 9, 10, 11, 12 and 13 divisions; finally the *Group5* is underlying the plot area reserved for the results of the tests using configurations of five building parts, each one holding 11, 12, 13, 14 and 15 divisions

unique acyclic path which ensure the connectivity of the divisions inside the virtual buildings. Thus, a building with 10 divisions contains 9 transitions which is the minimum value to provide reachability among those divisions. The chosen roof for each generation trial was the flat type in order to minimize the number of roof vertices and to provide a fairer comparison between structures under this same condition. Plot 7.9 depicts these tests.

The previous plot reveals that the average CPU usage stabilized between 37 and 61 % during the tests. The interval of RAM consumption is about [40, 45] MB. It is also notorious that the most complex structure—with 25,728 vertices—took no longer than 125 ms to be generated. Moreover, the generation of the most basic one—composed by 5522 vertices—took 15 ms. Such results seems to point out the agility of the presented procedural modelling methodology which is capable of generating structures of considerable complexity within acceptable time ranges and using plausible computational resources.

7.8 Summary

A toolkit implementing the final version of the procedural modelling methodology addressed in this book was used to generate virtual building models for evaluation, pointing out the methodology flexibility and validating its implementation, by producing a large variety of random structures while ensuring coherency.

Based on the presented results, it was demonstrated that this methodology is capable of producing virtual buildings confined by arbitrary convex shapes and also fake-concave shapes, using a method that flags geometric holes. This fake-concave method is appropriated for producing L-shaped or U-shaped buildings.

Moreover, the process for inner wall adaptation seems to be suitable and effective to define the number of inner wall segments that constraint a given division. There is the possibility of generating divisions containing four to eight wall segments.

The subdividing process was also tested regarding its effectiveness. Treemap was pushed to divide several buildings constrained by arbitrary outline into divisions and holes. It became evident that the limit for splitting will only depend on the size of the constraint polygon, number of inner divisions and related dimensions.

The predictable nature of this treemap approach allowed the development of the stochastic process for fully automatic virtual buildings production. This process was applied to generate a set of buildings with different division sets, distinct arrangements and also with different types of constraint limits: convex, U-shaped and L-shaped. The related tests highlighted the process potential in generating several buildings with random formats and aleatory division sets, autonomously. Another addressed aspect was the extensibility of the specified generic ontology, which derived to the Roman architecture to demonstrate the flexibility and adaptability of such knowledge organization in the present methodology. A general purpose building was compared to a Roman *domus*. Without changing the methodology's core, the modeller was capable of producing virtual buildings with quite different structures. Finally, performance tests were carried out regarding the methodology implementation. It was demonstrated that simple structures with around 5500 vertices can be geometrically produced in a scarce 15 ms, while more complex structures composed by ≈25,700 vertices can be generated in less than 130 ms. These results seems to indicate that this procedural modelling methodology implementation is capable of performing building generations rapidly and using only a modest part of the available computational resources.

References

1. RGEU: Regulamento geral das edificações urbanas, decreto n.° 38382 (2008)
2. Rodrigues, N.: Rule-based generation of virtual traversable architectural-period houses. Ph.D. thesis, University of Trás-os-Montes e Alto Douro (2010)

Chapter 8
Conclusions

Abstract This last chapter succinctly reviews the main contributions of the procedural modelling methodology presented in this book, briefly compares some of its aspects with other works and presents a set of notes to be considered as future research opportunities.

8.1 Overall Summary

This book started with a literature review on ontologies for virtual environments and procedural modelling solutions that allowed the identification of some issues: the apparent lack of a robust standard-based virtual building ontology, capable of, at least, mapping the majority of real-world possibilities; the insufficiency of procedural modelling methodologies dealing with traversable buildings constrained by arbitrary shapes and composed by inner divisions also arbitrarily shaped. To overcome this issues, a flexible and extensible building ontology was designed and a procedural modelling methodology, guided by this ontology and matured throughout several development stages, was presented.

8.1.1 Building Ontology

The presented ontology was designed considering the suggestions given by CityGML standard [1, 2] and started of as being generic. That knowledge structure established that the *Building* is the major abstract container which is composed by one or more horizontal compositions displaced in the building's ground, also known as building parts. Every building part if formed by one or more floors, each one containing the interior divisions. The boundary surfaces represent the walls that delimit entities, such as divisions (interior isolation) and floors (exterior isolation). Finally, transitions representing the traversable points and other types of boundary openings—like doors and windows—are directly related to the building and abstract building elements (divisions and floors).

© The Author(s) 2016
T. Adão et al., *Ontology-based Procedural Modelling of Traversable Buildings Composed by Arbitrary Shapes*, SpringerBriefs in Computer Science,
DOI 10.1007/978-3-319-42372-2_8

Afterwards, the roman architecture was used to demonstrate how to derive the generic ontology. The main knowledge structure is always maintained, while extending the elements into particular classes. For example, a *Building* extends to *Roman-Building* which, in turn, can be extended to a *Domus*, *Theatre*, *Forum* and so on. Moreover, particular building parts or divisions can extend from the generic *BuildingPart* or *Division*, respectively. For example *Peristylium*, *Culina* and *Cubiculum* are roman rooms that inherit features from the generic *Division*. The *AbstractElement* is an ontological entity planned to support the extension to concrete structures. In the case of the roman architecture, arches and columns are represented as inherited structures from the generic *AbstractElement* class. Every other architectonic style can be described through the same extension mechanism.

Besides the structuring of building elements, the ontology also performs an important role in the procedural modelling methodology regulation, summed up in the following subsection.

8.1.2 *Procedural Modelling Methodology*

The generic procedural modelling methodology for the generation of virtual buildings was present since the beginning of this book. According to it, a virtual building model is achieved by: first, determine a floor plan; then, connected divisions; afterwards, extrude the walls, generate the roof and create the final elements, such as footers and transitions. However, this generic methodology progressed from chapter to chapter, as it was being enhanced and improved. In fact, while the earlier chapters presented a process capable of producing virtual buildings only with square geometries, further on it was already possible to subdivide constraint convex polygons and to define geometric holes (fake-concave constraint polygons). Another improvement was the possibility of defining the number of inner wall segments of a division which implicitly assumes a shape based on this definition. Moreover, the flexibility of the presented procedural modelling methodology was demonstrated by generating two types of virtual structures (generic and roman). A stochastic process which takes advantage from the predictability and flexibility of the floor plan subdivision method—the treemap approach—was also established to demonstrate that the current methodology can also be used to produce buildings quickly and considering a minimalist set of inputs. So, summing up the different phases of the procedural modelling methodology

(A) Floor plan:
   The floor plan subdivision method relies in a treemap approach. The recursion attached to the method allowed the splitting of constraint building polygons into smaller areas to provide the proper division arrangements. Originally, treemap was used to deal with rectangles but it also proved effective in dividing other convex shapes beyond the rectangles. The generation of floor plans in this pro-

cedural modelling methodology also supports the adjustment of room shapes through the modification of delimiting wall segments.

(B) 3D virtual model:

The 3D models are achieved through a set of steps, applied after the floor plan subdivision: the inner walls and the facade walls are extruded to a given height; transitions, specifically doors and windows, are subjected to a similar extrusion process; each building part is then covered with a roof; and finally some model enhancements are made, such as the creation of footers, frames for windows and doors and thickening the roof skeleton. The resulting virtual buildings models provide a coherent visualization that allows to clearly distinguish the different building elements and architectonic style features. Virtual building models can be further enriched with the proper ontological extensions and geometrical implementations.

One final remark goes to the possibility of using the presented procedural modelling methodology for generating buildings, deterministic and stochastically. This methodology is mainly oriented for the deterministic generation of structures. The rules that feed the generation through XML or grammar are rigid values that do not consider alternatives for the building production, i.e. the same rules with the same parameters will always produce one single structure. However, the manageability of the methodology—namely at the treemap level approach—along with pseudorandom attributions for division arrangements, building part heights and other grammar parameters allowed the establishment of a stochastic process, thus enabling the use of this methodology for the fully automatic generation of buildings.

8.2 Discussion and Future Directions

A wide variety of solutions regarding the procedural modelling of virtual buildings with interiors has been proposed by some authors, as for example [3–7] with interesting automation processes (e.g. computer-generated floor plans) and results. However, most of them confine the building's geometries to squares. Other works, such as those proposed by Hohmann et al. [8] and Leblanc et al. [9] opted for using CSG algorithms and generative modelling languages to explore their great potential to generate complex structures. Those approaches, which require programming skills and are usually very time consuming, were also applied to produce traversable buildings, mainly composed by rectangular shapes. Regarding the shapes' arbitrariness, only the work developed by Dahl and Rinde [10] was found during this book literature review. These authors proposed a solution for generating building structures constrained by non-rectangular geometric shapes. However, the interior divisions' generation carried out by the algorithm does not seem to be appropriate when rooms' generation control (for example geometric constraints and rooms' arrangements) is required. Dahl and Rinde [10] also document the impossibility of dealing with building limits containing geometric holes. In addition, texturing is an absent feature, making impossible the visual distinction between room types.

Moreover, despite the straight orientation of CityGML for urban environments, the standard remains almost unused in procedural modelling approaches. Ontology-based solutions work with customized semantics or ontologies. Since CityGML constitutes the standard for virtual urban environments validated and released by a consortium, it was preferred as a base for the creation of the regulatory ontology for buildings that intends to fit a wider range of structures present in real world.

Considering the aforementioned, a new ontology-based procedural modelling methodology was presented resulting in a set of achievements

- the presented methodology is capable of producing traversable buildings constrained by arbitrary convex shapes;
- a process to change the format of the interior rooms was achieved through the wall number modification;
- a "fake-concave" technique was properly adapted to support non-convex buildings layouts;
- an extensible CityGML-based building ontology to guide the procedural modelling process and to support the generation of other architectural style buildings (e.g. roman houses) was designed and implemented within the methodology context;
- some ontology-based structures—data model and grammar—were established as input formats (definition rules institution);
- finally, a computer managed processes regarding the stochastic generation was implemented to automatize buildings' production.

A procedural modelling methodology evaluation was carried out to attest the accomplishments listed above. Summing up, the presented procedural modelling methodology complies with the objectives and main contributions that were defined in this book. However, a set of further enhancements and improvements that can be done to the presented procedural modelling methodology were identified to be addressed as future work, namely

- Support to multiple floors: the designed ontology for buildings foresees the possibility of having multiple floors. However, the presented procedural modelling methodology requires a few modifications to support the generation of buildings with more than a ground floor. At least, a workaround can be achieved based on the establishment of some assumptions, for example

    - in multi-floor buildings, usually only the ground floor is a different from all others, while the remaining ones are replicas from the first floor;
    - the different floors are connected through a common aligned element which provides access to the different levels (an elevator or a staircase).

- Development of mechanisms capable of rapidly adapt the methodology for the production of precise and faithful buildings compliant with real-world architectural rules;

- Support to pure concave geometries: currently, the fake-concave technique is enough to produce buildings with geometric holes. However, a pure concave approach (e.g. ear-clipping) could be an interesting comparison feature;
- Reuse of divisions' dead zones: division wall's adaptation results in dead zones (or blank zones) that currently contribute to the waste of buildings' useful area. To address this issue, some resolutions can be considered. A possibility could pass by reinjecting the wasted area of those dead zones into the divisions that borrowed spaces during the floor plan probing stage. One might also consider the relaxation of some restrictions to adapt a building's constraint shape to the divisions' shapes with a goal of removing those death zones or even to arrange the divisions' walls segments in a more advantageous format aiming the reduction of space waste;
- Development of a tool for geometric customization: the geometric kit developed for the presented methodology is extensive and flexible. However, the production of geometry for each ontological object is programmer dependent. The integration of a GUI-based tool for customizing shapes would enable this independence, passing the appearance responsibilities to the designers and final users;
- Inclusion of furniture: the ontology enables the differentiation between divisions which can constitute a good starting point for the automatic placement of furniture, according to the different division types;
- Support to the modification of rules through a visual editor: currently, the developed software toolkit applies the methodology to create virtual models for visualization that cannot be changed without using a proper 3D software editor. Thus, seems pertinent to improve this toolkit by making it capable of adapting user modifications upon the post-generated 3D models with real-time repercussions in definition rules, interactively.

To conclude, it is hoped that this book can contribute to the improvement of Procedural Modelling field, opening doors for new processes, methods and techniques besides the ones that were presented.

References

1. Gröger, G., Kolbe, T.H., Czerwinski, A., Nagel, C.: OGC City Geography Markup Language (CityGML) Encoding Standard. Technical report, Open Geospatial Consortium (2008)
2. Gröger, G., Kolbe, T.H., Nagel, C., Häfele, K.-H.: OGC City Geography Markup Language (CityGML) Encoding Standard. Technical report, Open Geospatial Consortium (2012)
3. Martin, J.: Algorithmic beauty of buildings methods for procedural building generation. Computer Science Honors Theses, p. 4 (2005)
4. Hahn, E., Bose, P., Whitehead, A.: Lazy generation of building interiors in realtime. In: Canadian Conference on Electrical and Computer Engineering, 2006, CCECE '06, pp. 2441–2444, May 2006. doi:10.1109/CCECE.2006.277767
5. Merrell, P., Schkufza, E., Koltun, V.: Computer-generated residential building layouts. ACM Trans. Graph. 29(6), 181:1–181:12 (2010). ISSN 0730-0301. doi:10.1145/1882261.1866203
6. Marson, F., Raupp Musse, S.: Automatic real-time generation of floor plans based on squarified treemaps algorithm. Int. J. Comput. Games Technol. 2010, 7:1–7:10 (2010). ISSN 1687-7047. doi:10.1155/2010/624817

Index

© The Author(s) 2016
T. Adão et al., *Ontology-based Procedural Modelling of Traversable Buildings Composed by Arbitrary Shapes*, SpringerBriefs in Computer Science, DOI 10.1007/978-3-319-42372-2

Printed in the United States
By Bookmasters